WORLD CHAMPIONS

THE STORY OF THE
DENVER BRONCOS
THIRD NFL CHAMPIONSHIP

Nicky Brillowski, Book and Cover Design

ISBN: 978-1-940056-37-1

Printed in the United States of America
KCI Sports Publishing   3340 Whiting Avenue, Suite 5   Stevens Point, WI 54481
Phone: 1-800-697-3756   Fax: 715-344-2668
www.kcisports.com

CONTENTS

Peyton Manning, right, and head coach Gary Kubiak celebrate after their win against the Carolina Panthers. *AP Photo*

Denver Broncos — World Champions!

Broncos fans have waited 18 long years to utter those words, but the Broncos are finally back on top.

Denver 24 Carolina 10

This was a victory that had been months in the making. Following the Broncos early exit from the 2014 playoffs, GM John Elway headed into the offseason with one goal in mind—building a team that could win Super Bowl 50.

Mission accomplished.

On their way to Super Bowl 50 this Broncos team overcame a series of injuries that gutted the roster and landed seven players on injured reserve. They overcame the loss of Hall of Fame quarterback Peyton Manning for six games and twice weathered back-to-back regular season losses by responding with hard-fought victories the following week.

The perseverance, teamwork and will to win that made up the DNA of this Broncos team was on full display week after week, resulting in a season of highlights, including Bradley Robey's 21-yard fumble return for a touchdown with :27 seconds left to beat Kansas City. Or the complete dismantling of the Aaron Rodgers-led offense in the dominating Sunday night win over Green Bay. Or Brandon McManus' 37-yard field goal in overtime to beat pesky Cincinnati.

And who will ever forget the AFC Championship win over Tom Brady and the Patriots? The official game attendance was 77,112, but that number may well grow over the years as Broncos fans happily reminisce about that "I was there" game for years to come.

Our heartfelt congratulations go out to the Bowlen family, GM John Elway, Coach Gary Kubiak and his staff, and the entire team on their accomplishments this season. To Peyton Manning, we say thanks for so many great memories. If this was indeed your last rodeo, we wish you all the best.

To the Denver fans, we hope you'll enjoy the memories of a wonderful season we share here. And we hope to be able to do the same thing for you again next year.

Sincerely,

KCI Sports Publishing

John Elway holds up the Vince Lombardi trophy during the postgame celebration. *AP Photo*

7

Baltimore quarterback Joe Flacco
(5) is sacked by Broncos linebacker
DeMarcus Ware (94). *AP Photo*

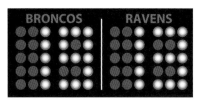

vs. Baltimore Ravens, Sept. 13
Sports Authority Field at Mile High
Denver, Colorado

DEFENSE LEADS WAY IN SEASON OPENER

Thanks to Denver's dazzling defense, Peyton Manning is celebrating a record 13th season-opening win, 19-13 over the Baltimore Ravens on Sunday in a slugfest Gary Kubiak said "might be the greatest defensive football game I've ever been a part of as a coach."

Manning was 24 of 40 for 175 yards and his four sacks were his most since his emotional homecoming at Indy in 2013. Asked to grade his performance, he said, "I'm going with fair," an assessment that the fans at Sports Authority Field might consider generous judging by their own harsh reactions.

Offenses, though, don't always have to do the heavy lifting, said Broncos safety Aqib Talib, who scored Denver's only touchdown.

"I think John Elway had like 115 yards and won the Super Bowl one time, so it's definitely possible," Talib said.

Manning managed just 150 net yards, but that was 50 more than Joe Flacco in a game in which neither team ran a play inside their opponents' 20 until 3:50 remained.

Counting the preseason, the NFL's career touchdown champion has yet to find the goal line in 21 drives.

The ground games weren't much better: Baltimore gained 73 yards, Denver 69, in a grind-it-out game that sent many players limping to the sideline or off on carts. The casualty list included Terrell Suggs (torn Achilles) and line judge Gary Arthur broke a collarbone.

Denver Broncos cornerback Aqib Talib (21) returns an interception for a touchdown. *AP Photo*

The unveiling of Denver's new mashup offense merging Manning's defensive deciphering skills with Kubiak's run-oriented philosophies was largely a dud — bounced passes, overthrows, four sacks, a false start on No. 18 himself — until, that is, he directed a 17-play drive that ate up 81 yards and almost 11 minutes in the fourth quarter. It ended with Brandon McManus' fourth field goal.

"To me that resembled more of the Kubiak offense, chipping away, wearing guys down," said former Ravens tight end Owen Daniels. "Good to do that against a team that prides itself on being physical and being bullies."

Safety Darian Stewart, who also followed Kubiak to Denver, snatched the ball from tight end Crockett Gillmore in the end zone with 28 seconds left to seal the win for the four-time defending AFC West champs.

"That's my old team and it was just good to go out there and finally get to hit them," Stewart said.

Cornerback Jimmy Smith's 24-yard pick-6 was Baltimore's only touchdown and Talib responded with a 51-yard interception return for a TD that put Denver ahead for good, 16-13.

Manning was playing behind an O-line with four new players, two of whom made their NFL debut. But he wasn't about to dissect the offense's performance, testily insisting, "no matter how many times you ask it, this is not three different teams we have here. We don't have a Broncos offensive team, a Broncos defensive team and a Broncos special teams.

"The Broncos beat the Ravens today. There's your summary right there."

The only points in the first half came through the uprights with McManus kicking three field goals from 57, 56 and 43 yards, and Justin Tucker kicking a 52-yarder for Baltimore.

The Broncos won for just the second time in 23 years when not scoring a touchdown. The last time they managed to do it was Sept. 17, 2006, when they beat the Chiefs. 9-6.

"You better be able to win this way in this league," Kubiak said. "It's just too tough a league."■

BOX SCORE

	1	2	3	4	T
Baltimore	0	3	10	0	13
Denver	6	3	7	3	19

GAME LEADERS

PASSING YARDS
BAL	J. Flacco	18-32, 117 YDS, 2 INT
DEN	P. Manning	24-40, 175 YDS, 1 INT

RUSHING YARDS
BAL	J. Forsett	14 CAR, 43 YDS
DEN	R. Hillman	12 CAR, 41 YDS

RECEIVING YARDS
BAL	M. Brown	2 REC, 25 YDS
DEN	E. Sanders	8 REC, 65 YDS

Denver linebackers Brandon Marshall (54) and Danny Trevathan (59) celebrate a sack. *AP Photo*

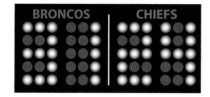

BRONCOS | **CHIEFS**

at Kansas City Chiefs, Sept. 17
Arrowhead Stadium
Kansas City, Missouri

BRONCOS STUN CHIEFS

Peyton Manning and the Denver Broncos have beaten the Kansas City Chiefs every way imaginable over the years, from playoff shootouts to defensive tug-of-wars.

Well, not quite every way. Not until Thursday night.

Denver cornerback Bradley Roby returned Jamaal Charles' second fumble 21 yards for a touchdown with 27 seconds left, completing a stunning comeback in the closing minute for a 31-24 victory — the Broncos' seventh straight over their AFC West rivals.

"I'm not quite sure I'd ever been in one quite like that," Manning said. "That was a new one."

Manning threw for 256 yards and three scores, the last to Emmanuel Sanders with 36 seconds left as the Broncos (2-0) appeared to force overtime. But on the next play from scrimmage, with the Chiefs (1-1) also eyeing overtime, Charles was stripped by Brandon Marshall and the ball bounced right into Roby's hands.

The dramatic about-face came after Knile Davis gave Kansas City the lead with 2:27 left on an 8-yard run, raising hope among a sellout crowd that the Chiefs might finally end some curses.

Instead, Denver won its 13th straight division road game, breaking a tie with the San Francisco 49ers (1987-90) for most in NFL history. And for one night, Manning

Broncos receiver Emmanuel Sanders (10) leaps into the end zone to complete a 16-yard touchdown reception during the second quarter. *AP Photo*

quieted his growing doubters by improving to 14-1 in his career against the Chiefs.

"I've been involved in a couple of pretty crazy games," he said, "but nothing quite like this."

Charles finished with 125 yards rushing and a touchdown, but he will only remember his fumbles — one in the red zone early in the game, the other deep in his own territory late in the game.

"I have to be careful with the ball," Charles said. "It's my fault."

Alex Smith threw for 191 yards for Kansas City, but also had two passes picked off.

Manning threw a pick-six of his own, but he responded when it mattered the most.

The Broncos took over at their own 20 after Davis had given Kansas City the lead, and the seven-time All-Pro marched them calmly down field. Manning found Demaryius Thomas for three long receptions to get deep into Chiefs territory, then hit Sanders with a strike over the middle on third-and-10 from the Chiefs 19 for the touchdown that kept Denver alive.

"That last drive was really good," said Manning, who joined Brett Favre during the game as the only quarterbacks in NFL history with at least 70,000 yards passing. "I'm really proud of our young offensive line — no poise issues, no communication issues."

The late-game dramatics transpired after the Chiefs bolted to a 14-0 lead in their home-opener, energizing a boisterous, red-clad crowd that had been tailgating all afternoon.

But like he has so often against the Chiefs, Manning answered by leading Denver on an 80-yard TD march late in the first half. The capper was a pass over the middle to Sanders, who slipped between the

safeties and somersaulted into the end zone for the 16-yard touchdown reception.

Two plays later, Aqib Talib picked off Smith's throw on a poorly thrown pass in the flat, and the Broncos needed just four plays for Manning to find Virgil Green with a tying touchdown toss.

After swapping field goals, the Chiefs were poised to celebrate when Davis took a handoff from Smith as the quarterback fell down and raced into the end zone late in the fourth quarter.

Turned out to be not late enough for Manning and the Broncos.

"I'll tell you," Manning said, "their defense is so much better than last year. They're so stout against the run. They just make it hard all night. We just kept plugging." ∎

BOX SCORE

	1	2	3	4	T
Denver	0	14	3	14	31
Kansas City	0	14	3	7	24

GAME LEADERS

PASSING YARDS
DEN	P. Manning	26-45, 256 YDS, 3 TD, 1 INT
KC	A. Smith	16-25, 191 YDS, 2 INT

RUSHING YARDS
DEN	R. Hillman	9 CAR, 34 YDS
KC	J. Charles	21 CAR, 125 YDS, 1 TD

RECEIVING YARDS
DEN	D. Thomas	8 REC, 116 YDS
KC	T. Kelce	4 REC, 58 YDS

Quarterback Peyton Manning (18) passes over the outstretched arm of Chiefs linebacker Justin Houston (50). *AP Photo*

Chiefs quarterback Alex Smith (11) is taken down for a sack by Broncos defensive tackle Malik Jackson (97) and linebacker Von Miller (58). *AP Photo*

Quarterback Peyton Manning (18) unloads a 45-yard touchdown pass to Demaryius Thomas with :05 left in the first half. *AP Photo*

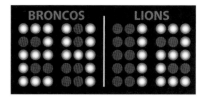

BRONCOS	LIONS

at Detroit Lions, Sept. 27
Ford Field
Detroit, Michigan

MANNING LEADS BRONCOS PAST LIONS

Peyton Manning was cool and confident, lofting passes to teammates as if they were buddies in his backyard.

Whether it was third or fourth down, in the second or fourth quarter, the 39-year-old Manning showed he still has it.

Manning converted a fourth down with a 45-yard touchdown pass to Demaryius Thomas with 5 seconds left in the first half. Then he threw an 11-yard scoring pass to Owen Daniels on a third down with 2:28 remaining, lifting the Denver Broncos to a 24-12 victory over the Detroit Lions on Sunday night.

He credited the coaching staff with using a pistol formation, giving him the ball in a short shotgun with a running back behind him, after he was under center for some snaps during the first two games.

"I imagine it will be part of the arsenal throughout the season," Manning said. "It gave us some help in protection."

Manning was sacked only once after he was sacked seven times in the first two games, helping him more than double his longest pass of the year on his 45-yard pass to Thomas.

"We protected him better than we have," Denver coach Gary Kubiak said.

Manning was 31 of 42 for 324 yards with two TDs and an interception. He and Brett Favre are the only players in NFL history with at least 6,000 completions.

The last time the Broncos (3-0) won their

Tight end Owen Daniels (81) hauls in a 11-yard touchdown pass. *AP Photo*

first three games was in 2013, when they reached the Super Bowl.

Aqib Talib blocked an extra-point kick by former Bronco Matt Prater early in the second quarter to keep Denver's one-point lead. The Broncos also stopped a 2-point conversion run, keeping them ahead 14-12 early in the third quarter.

Stafford had three turnovers, including a fumble and interception at midfield in the fourth quarter. He might've had a good reason to be rattled because DeMarcus Ware was in on two sacks and he was hit and hurried throughout Detroit's home opener.

Broncos running back C.J. Anderson left in the first half to be evaluated for a concussion, but was cleared and returned in the second half.

Thomas had nine receptions for 92 yards and a lead-padding score in which he outleaped Darius Slay to snatch the football out of the air. He celebrated by backpedaling into the end zone, drawing an unsportsmanlike conduct penalty.

Stafford was 31 of 45 for 282 yards with a 16-yard TD pass to Ameer Abdullah in the third quarter, two interceptions and a fumble on a play in which he had at least once chance to throw the ball away. Calvin Johnson had eight receptions for 77 yards and drew a pass-interference penalty against Talib in the end zone to set up Joique Bell's 1-yard leap over a pile of lineman.

It looked as if Detroit's defense was going to prevent the Broncos from taking advantage of Stafford's second turnover, but it negated a missed field goal by being in an illegal formation.

Denver got 5 yards closer and Brandon McManus made the field goal to give the Broncos a five-point lead.

Stafford then tried to force a pass to Johnson and safety David Bruton Jr. dropped into a zone to pick off the pass he tipped to himself with his right hand, then returned 12 yards.

"Our responsibility is get to the ball on defense," Bruton said.

Moments later, Manning lofted a 34-yard pass to Emmanuel Sanders, who outjumped Slay, to set up his throw that only the 6-foot-3 Daniels could catch in the end zone. ∎

BOX SCORE

	1	2	3	4	T
Denver	0	14	0	10	24
Detroit	0	6	6	0	12

GAME LEADERS

PASSING YARDS
DEN P. Manning 31-42, 324 YDS, 2 TD, 1 INT
DET M. Stafford 31-45, 282 YDS, 1 TD, 2 INT

RUSHING YARDS
DEN C.J. Anderson 8 CAR, 18 YDS
DET A. Abdullah 8 CAR, 23 YDS

RECEIVING YARDS
DEN D. Thomas 9 REC, 92 YDS, 1 TD
DET C. Johnson 8 REC, 77 YDS

Lions receiver Calvin Johnson (81) goes up for a pass in the end zone as Broncos cornerback Aqib Talib (21) defends. *AP Photo*

Broncos linebacker Von Miller (58) celebrates after sacking Vikings quarterback Teddy Bridgewater (5) during second half action. *AP Photo*

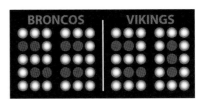

vs. Minnesota Vikings, Oct. 4
Sports Authority Field at Mile High
Denver, Colorado

BRONCOS D DOMINATES IN 23-20 WIN

Bursting through the line for jaw-dropping plays is quickly becoming the Denver Broncos' calling card.

Only this time, the offense joined the party that's been "pass rushers only" until Sunday.

Ronnie Hillman raced around the left sideline on a classic stretch play for a 72-yard touchdown run, and the league's top-ranked defense collected seven more sacks in a 23-20 victory over the Minnesota Vikings.

"We had three bad weeks of running the ball and tonight we got it started," Hillman said after his third career 100-yard game. "This week it was just me and C.J. (Anderson) got tired of everyone trying to tell us that we can't run the ball."

The unbeaten Broncos (4-0) revved up their ground game behind Hillman and it came in handy on a day the Vikings (2-2) picked off Peyton Manning twice and turned the takeaways into 10 points.

The Broncos came into the game averaging just 57 yards rushing. With Manning in the pistol formation behind a patchwork offensive line and two tight ends lined up on the left side, Hillman went left, gathered in Manning's pitch, hit the crease and was gone down the sideline.

It was the longest touchdown run by a Broncos running back in 15 years.

"I knew nobody was going to catch him," teammate Demaryius Thomas said. "I was happy. It's good for the offense, gives guys confidence we can hit those long runs."

Hillman finished with 103 yards on 11 carries for his third career 100-yard game.

Denver's top-ranked defense limited Adrian Peterson to 81 yards on 16 carries - when Peterson was the MVP in 2012, his lowest output was 86 yards against the Texans and Wade Phillips, now Denver's defensive coordinator.

Peterson did get a 48-yard touchdown run on fourth-

Broncos running back Ronnie Hillman celebrates with the fans after scoring on a 72-yard touchdown run. *AP Photo*

and-inches to pull Minnesota to 20-17 with 10 minutes left. Cornerback Aqib Talib was right there in the middle, but had already turned his hips and by the time he turned back, Peterson was by him.

"That's just 'AP,'" Von Miller said. "We came into the game knowing that he was going to make plays and we're fortunate that that was the only big one."

Free safety Harrison Smith's interception two plays later set up Blair Walsh's tying field goal from 33 yards with 5:11 remaining.

Manning drove the Broncos 55 yards in nine plays, and Brandon McManus's 39-yard field goal with 1:51 left broke the tie.

"You have to have a short-term memory in this league," Manning said of bouncing back from his two turnovers. "On both occasions we responded the next series with scoring drives."

Then, Denver's defense went to work to close out another game.

Peterson missed the block on T.J. Ward and Miller smothered the loose football after the blitzing safety's sack-strip of Bridgewater at midfield with 29 seconds left.

"Definitely frustrating, especially when I feel like it's my fault," Peterson said, explaining Ward was hidden behind linebacker Brandon Marshall. "(I've) got to come through and make that block for Teddy."

All four of Denver's wins have come down to the closing minutes.

"I don't even think of it as close anymore," Miller said. "That's just how we play. It's just how football is. You stop thinking about the days when we would put up 40 and 50 (points) on teams. This is the National Football League and we're playing tough teams every week.

"I don't want to call it close because that's just how it's going to be in this league. It was another great game for us."∎

BOX SCORE

	1	2	3	4	T
Minnesota	0	10	0	10	20
Denver	3	10	7	3	23

GAME LEADERS

PASSING YARDS

MIN	T. Bridgewater	27-41, 269 YDS, 1 TD
DEN	P. Manning	17-27, 213 YDS, 1 TD, 2 INT

RUSHING YARDS

MIN	A. Peterson	16 CAR, 81 YDS, 1 TD
DEN	R. Hillman	11 CAR, 103 YDS, 1 TD

RECEIVING YARDS

MIN	S. Diggs	6 REC, 87 YDS
DEN	D. Thomas	9 REC, 93 YDS

Vikings quarterback Teddy Bridgewater (5) is smothered by Broncos defenders Von Miller (58), DeMarcus Ware (94) and Malik Jackson (97). *AP Photo*

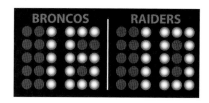

BRONCOS	RAIDERS

at Oakland Raiders, Oct. 11
O.co Coliseum
Oakland, California

HARRIS' INT LEADS BRONCOS PAST RAIDERS

After spending most of his career carrying his team to wins, Peyton Manning is just along for the ride this year with Denver.

Chris Harris Jr. returned a fourth-quarter interception 74 yards for a touchdown and the Broncos overcame a shaky day from Manning to beat the Oakland Raiders 16-10 on Sunday.

"You never know who it's going to be, but we've got a team full of play-makers on defense," Harris said. "If we got to win on D, we feel we can do it."

They've done it so far with 22 sacks, 14 turnovers and three defensive touchdowns as Manning and the offense have struggled for long stretches.

Manning has more interceptions (seven) than TD passes (six) through five games for the first time since his rookie season. He was intercepted twice by 1998 draft classmate Charles Woodson and failed to lead the Broncos (5-0) to an offensive touchdown for the second time in five games.

"We want to play better offensively," Manning said. "We want to do our job. Somehow, some way it's about getting the Denver Broncos a win. There's no question offensively we want to play

Denver cornerback Chris Harris Jr (25) celebrates after returning a fourth quarter interception 74 yards for the touchdown.
AP Photo

Broncos receiver Emmanuel Sanders extends to catch one of his nine receptions on the day. *AP Photo*

better. ... Everybody wants to do a better job and that starts with me."

Derek Carr threw for 249 yards and a 3-yard TD pass to Marcel Reece for the Raiders (2-3) but was done in by the interception midway through the fourth quarter with Oakland in position for a possible go-ahead field goal.

But Carr's third-down pass over the middle was off target and Harris picked it off and returned it for the score, silencing what had been a loud crowd in Oakland.

The Raiders added a late 50-yard field goal by Sebastian Janikowski but Denver recovered the onside kick to seal it.

Manning finished 22 for 35 for 266 yards but was sacked twice and had two interceptions. Denver ran for only 43 yards but used Harris' interception return and a sack-fumble by Von Miller that set up a field goal to beat the Raiders. This was Denver's second-lowest scoring regular season with Manning as quarterback, ahead of only a seven-point effort last year against St. Louis.

"We got to get better offensively," coach Gary Kubiak said. "The sad thing is we do some good stuff and we don't finish anything. That's what's disappointing. Then it all keeps going back to (Manning). That's not fair."

Before Harris' big play, the highlight of the game had been the play of Woodson, who turned 39 on Wednesday. Woodson, who beat Manning out for the Heisman Trophy in 1997, talked earlier in the week about wanting to get his first interception against Manning.

He ended up with two, becoming the oldest player in NFL history with more than one interception in a game.

"Those things are the shiny things, the shiny toys that you like, but it's about wins and losses," Woodson said.

Janikowski missed his second field goal of the game from 40 yards after Woodson's second interception, costing Oakland a shot at the lead. Janikowski also had a 38-yard attempt blocked by Sylvester Williams in the first quarter.■

BOX SCORE

	1	2	3	4	T
Denver	0	3	6	7	16
Oakland	0	7	0	3	10

GAME LEADERS

PASSING YARDS
DEN	P. Manning	22-35, 266 YDS, 2 INT
OAK	D. Carr	26-39, 249 YDS, 1 TD, 1 INT

RUSHING YARDS
DEN	C.J. Anderson	11 CAR, 22 YDS
OAK	L. Murray	13 CAR, 39 YDS

RECEIVING YARDS
DEN	E. Sanders	9 REC, 111 YDS
OAK	M. Crabtree	4 REC, 54 YDS

Defensive end Derek Wolfe (95) starts to celebrate after Oakland quarterback Derek Carr (4) is stripped of the ball by Broncos linebacker Von Miller (58) on a third quarter play. The fumble recovery gave the Broncos the ball on the Raiders 16-yard line. *AP Photo*

Is Von Miller the next coming of perennial All-Pro Lawrence Taylor?

Watching Miller get low, race around the edge and make New England Patriots offensive tackle Marcus Cannon look silly in the AFC Championship Game it's not hard to see why he draws comparisons to Lawrence Taylor.

Miller, the Denver Broncos star linebacker, is the best natural edge pass rusher in the NFL. It was on full display for the entire nation when the Broncos beat the Patriots to reach Super Bowl 50. Miller had 2.5 sacks in that contest and countless other pressures.

Miller is the best player on the NFL's best defense because of his combination of speed, flexibility and an increasingly complex arsenal of moves. Paired with veteran pass rusher DeMarcus Ware in coordinator Wade Phillips' aggressive defense, Miller dipped, spun and bullrushed his way to 11 of the Broncos' league-high 52 sacks.

Miller's play has reminded many of the legendary Taylor, a monster off the edge for the Giants who will be honored as one of the greatest players in Super Bowl history during the 50th edition of the game. Taylor had double-digit-sack seasons from 1984-90. He had 20.5 sacks in 1986, when he won the first of his two Super Bowls with the Giants.

Taylor averaged 11.0 sacks per season in his Hall of Fame career. Miller has averaged 12.0 in his first five professional seasons. And it would've been even higher if not for a drug suspension and injuries that limited him to nine games in the 2013 season.

The comparisons have Miller blushing and out of his comfort zone.

"It's humbling. Comparisons to guys like that make you uncomfortable," Miller said. "He's a Hall of Famer. I'm not comfortable with comparisons like that."

Maybe he should start getting comfortable with them. Miller, 26, is just getting started. There's nothing to suggest the string of sacks won't continue despite constant double teams.

Miller is set to become a free agent this offseason, but he's not going anywhere. The Broncos are not letting a player of his ability walk. Miller is an L.T.-like talent. It's why he was drafted No. 2 overall by the Broncos in the 2011 NFL Draft.

Those off-field concerns and injury questions feel like ages ago now. Miller, while still a goofball, has matured. He's out of the NFL's drug program thanks to two years of clean tests. And while he still leans on veteran teammate Ware for guidance, he's become a locker room leader thanks to his practice habits. Miller missed just one practice all season when he had a bad reaction to some movie theater mozzarella sticks in January.

"I just think he had a tremendous amount of support — not just from us, but in his personal life, from his mom and dad. His agent's done a tremendous job getting him in the right situation and around the right people," Broncos general manager John Elway said. "But the bottom line is, you can have all the support and everything you could want, (but) unless you make your mind up that that's what you want to do, it'll never happen.

"Really all the credit goes to Von, because he made his mind up what he wanted to be ... It's been a tremendous maturation process for him, and we're thrilled that he's come through."

And despite being 1 year old the last time Taylor notched a double-digit-sack season, Miller understands what that means to be compared to perhaps the greatest defensive player of all time.

"I know a lot about him," Miller said. "You're talking about Lawrence Taylor, one of the greatest linebackers to ever the play the game."

What exactly are the similarities between the two?

"We get sacks," Miller said with a laugh. "We get sacks."∎

Denver kicker Brandon McManus (8) drills a 34-yard field goal to defeat Cleveland in overtime. *AP Photo*

DENVER BRONCOS

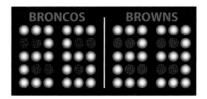

BRONCOS	BROWNS

at Cleveland Browns, Oct. 18
FirstEnergy Stadium
Cleveland, Ohio

MCMANUS FG GIVES BRONCOS OT WIN

The top-ranked defense in the NFL was at its best when it had to be on Sunday to keep the Denver Broncos undefeated with a hard-earned 26-23 overtime victory over the Cleveland Browns.

Brandon McManus booted a 35-yard field goal with 4:56 remaining in overtime after the Broncos defense sacked quarterback Josh McCown twice on the Browns only possession of overtime.

The lead changed hands twice in the fourth quarter before a 26-yard field goal by Browns kicker Travis Coons with 1:30 to play tied the score, 23-23.

Broncos quarterback Peyton Manning threw a 75-yard touchdown pass to wide receiver Emmanuel Sanders midway through the fourth quarter one play after the Browns took the lead for the first time after being down 10-0 at halftime.

The Browns scored three touchdowns in the second half and took a 20-16 lead with 8:07 to play on a 35-yard interception return by linebacker Karlos Dansby.

The interception was the second of the game thrown by Manning, but just when it seemed all the momentum was with the Browns, the Broncos' 39-year-old quarterback hooked up with Sanders to temporarily regain the lead for Denver at 23-20. It was the first touchdown by the offense in 26 possessions.

"We're not playing as well as we'd like, but we're playing well enough," Manning

Browns running back Duke Johnson (29) is sent airborne by Broncos cornerback Aqib Talib (21). *AP Photo*

said. "We're doing some things right at critical times when we have to whether it's the last drive of the game or overtime."

A 29-yard field goal by McManus accounted for the only scoring of the first quarter. He finished the day with four field goals in five attempts and knew the game would come down to him in overtime.

"During warm-ups the balls were moving from one upright to the other," McManus said. "That's how windy it was. (The game-winner) didn't even move a yard. I'm excited I was able to overcome that miss and win this game."

The Browns started a drive on their own 19 late in the first quarter and advanced to the Denver 38 to start the second period. Running back Isaiah Crowell lost two yards on a run to the right. On second down, quarterback Josh McCown looked to his right for wide receiver Travis Benjamin, but Denver cornerback Aqib Talib jumped the route and sprinted 63 yards to the end zone with the Broncos' eighth interception of the season.

The Browns cut their 10-0 halftime deficit to a field goal with a touchdown on their first possession of the third quarter when McCown threw a 12-yard fade to tight end Gary Barnidge in

the back right corner of the end zone.

Twice in the third quarter after cutting the lead to 10-7 the Browns got the ball back with good field position but each time the Broncos refused to yield. One Cleveland possession beginning at the Browns 35 ended in a three-and-out and one that started at the Browns 48 ended with a strip sack by Broncos linebacker Shaq Barrett. Barrett recovered the fumble to set up a 25-yard field goal by McManus.

McManus kicked his third field goal of the game for a 16-7 lead and then the Browns cut it to 16-14 on a 14-yard touchdown pass to Barnidge with 9:20 left.∎

BOX SCORE

	1	2	3	4	OT	T
Denver	3	7	3	10	3	26
Cleveland	0	0	7	16	0	23

GAME LEADERS

PASSING YARDS
DEN P. Manning 26-48, 290 YDS, 1 TD, 3 INT
CLE J. McCown 20-39, 213 YDS, 2 TD, 2 INT

RUSHING YARDS
DEN R. Hillman 20 CAR, 111 YDS
CLE D. Johnson Jr. 9 CAR, 38 YDS

RECEIVING YARDS
DEN D. Thomas 10 REC, 111 YDS
CLE T. Benjamin 9 REC, 117 YDS

Broncos receiver Demaryius Thomas (88) reaches over Browns cornerback Pierre Desir (26) to make the catch. *AP Photo*

33

Green Bay tight end Richard Rodgers (82) is drilled by Broncos defenders Kayvon Webster (36), Chris Harris Jr. (25) and Malik Jackson (97). *AP Photo*

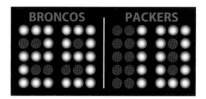

**vs. Green Bay Packers, Nov. 1
Sports Authority Field at Mile High
Denver, Colorado**

BRONCOS SHRED PACKERS 29-10

After plodding along for much of the season and having a stout defense carry the team, the Denver Broncos offense found its footing and roared to life.

Ronnie Hillman ran for two touchdowns and C.J. Anderson had another, and the Broncos used a bruising rushing attack and picked their spots passing to down Green Bay 29-10 Sunday night, remaining unbeaten and handing the Packers their first loss of the season.

With their running game clicking and helping to open up passing lanes, Peyton Manning threw for 340 yards. It was his 186th career regular-season win, tying Brett Favre for most victories by a starting quarterback in NFL history. Demaryius Thomas was his favorite target, with eight receptions for 168 yards, his team-record-tying 31st game with at least 100 yards receiving.

"Everybody on offense has been working hard to try to improve and play better and I thought we did that tonight," Manning said. "It proves when we do execute we are capable of making some big plays but you've got to do it every week."

The Broncos improved to 7-0 to start a season for just the second time in their history. They got off to a 13-0 start in 1998. Green Bay fell to 6-1, snapping an eight-game regular-season winning streak dating to last year.

Running back Ronnie Hillman (23) breaks free for a 15-yard touchdown run during the second quarter. *AP Photo*

Broncos linebacker DeMarcus Ware (94) sacks Green Bay quarterback Aaron Rodgers (12). The ensuing fumble was recovered in the end zone by Packers tight end Richard Rodgers (82) resulting in a safety. *AP Photo*

"They took advantage of us in the run game and the pass game," Packers cornerback Casey Hayward said.

Added Packers coach Mike McCarthy: "That was a humbling loss. I haven't had my butt kicked like that in a long time."

Denver's defense frustrated the Packers' high-powered offense, limiting Aaron Rodgers to 77 yards on 14 of 22 passing. He was sacked by DeMarcus Ware and fumbled early in the fourth quarter and in the scramble for the ball, it rolled into the end zone, where it was recovered by tight end Richard Rodgers for a safety.

Trailing 17-7 at the half, Green Bay pulled to within a touchdown on Mason Crosby's 56-yard field goal with 9:07 left in the third quarter.

But Denver regained separation behind their resurgent running game, which scored more rushing touchdowns against the Packers than it had in the previous six games (two). Anderson burst through a hole in the middle of the line and accelerated into the clear en route to a 28-yard touchdown and a 24-10 lead.

"We went out there wanting to make a statement," Broncos tight end Virgil Green said. "I feel like towards the end, we just had them. We

Broncos quarterback Peyton Manning (18) was on target all night going 21-29 for 340 yards passing. *AP Photo*

were manhandling them and I felt good about our execution."

Brandon McManus kicked his second field goal for the Broncos, a 24-yarder, with 12:25 remaining.

Denver bolted to a 17-0 lead — its biggest in a game this season — before a penalty-aided Packers drive culminated in running back Eddie Lacy's 2-yard touchdown run with 2:58 remaining in the second quarter to pull Green Bay to within 10 at the half.

Key completions by Manning helped set up Hillman's second scoring run. His 47-yard pass to Thomas set up a 15-yard scoring run by Hillman early in the second quarter and Thomas' 30-yard catch preceded Hillman's first TD run, covering 1 yard in the first quarter. ∎

BOX SCORE

	1	2	3	4	T
Green Bay	0	7	3	0	10
Denver	7	10	7	5	29

GAME LEADERS

PASSING YARDS
GB	A. Rodgers	14-22, 77 YDS
DEN	P. Manning	21-29, 340 YDS, 1 INT

RUSHING YARDS
GB	E. Lacy	11 CAR, 38 YDS, 1 TD
DEN	C.J. Anderson	14 CAR, 101 YDS, 1 TD

RECEIVING YARDS
GB	R. Cobb	6 REC, 27 YDS
DEN	D. Thomas	8 REC, 168 YDS

The name of Broncos owner Pat Bowlen is unveiled during his Broncos' Ring of Honor induction at halftime. *AP Photo*

Denver punt returner Omar Bolden (31) takes one back 83-yards for a touchdown on the final play of the first half. *AP Photo*

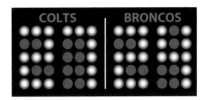

COLTS | BRONCOS

at Indianapolis Colts, Nov. 8
Lucas Oil Stadium
Idianapolis, Indiana

LUCK, COLTS GIVE BRONCOS FIRST LOSS

For Indianapolis quarterback Andrew Luck, the goal never was outplaying Colts legend Peyton Manning.

While he respects Manning and all of No. 18's lofty accomplishments, Luck has one mission: winning. Period.

Luck and the Colts spoiled the Denver Broncos' perfect season and Manning's potential record-setting day with a 27-24 victory Sunday in Lucas Oil Stadium.

Indianapolis led 17-0 in the second quarter, but Denver rallied to tie the game 17-17 in the third quarter and 24-24 in the middle of the fourth quarter.

Kicker Adam Vinatieri's 55-yard field goal with 6:13 remaining gave Indianapolis a three-point lead. The Colts drove 33 yard in seven plays, setting up the go-ahead score.

Reserve cornerback Darius Butler intercepted a Manning pass 13 seconds later, and Denver (7-1) never got the ball back.

Luck, who took over under center in Indianapolis after Manning was released following the 2011 season, completed 21 of 36 passes for 252 yards and two touchdowns.

Indianapolis improved to 4-5, breaking a three-game losing streak and taking sole possession of first place in the AFC South.

"Finally, we didn't shoot ourselves in the foot," said Luck, who struggled with turnovers and sacks

Colts quarterback Andrew Luck (12) takes a hard hit from Broncos linebacker Danny Trevathan (59). Luck suffered a lacerated kidney and torn abdominal muscle on the play. *AP Photo*

during the first eight games of the season. "The defense and special teams were great complementary pieces today."

Manning finished 21 of 36 for 281 yards, two touchdowns and two costly interceptions. Manning needed 284 passing yards to pass Brett Favre's NFL career record.

"When you don't play as well as you would like, it's hard to win on the road," Manning said. "We just didn't play well enough."

The victory, especially considering the Colts replaced offensive coordinator Pep Hamilton with associate head coach Rob Chudzinski on Tuesday after losing on Monday night in overtime at unbeaten Carolina, was special to head coach Chuck Pagano.

"This was a great team victory," Pagano said. "Peyton played great, but I am so proud of our guys. They never quit. They played 60 minutes. I love this team."

The Broncos tied the game at 24 with 8:54 to play on

BOX SCORE

	1	2	3	4	T
Denver	0	7	10	7	24
Indianapolis	7	10	0	10	27

GAME LEADERS

PASSING YARDS
DEN	P. Manning	21-36, 281 YDS, 2 TD, 2 INT
IND	A. Luck	21-36, 252 YDS, 2 TD

RUSHING YARDS
DEN	C.J. Anderson	7 CAR, 34 YDS
IND	F. Gore	28 CAR, 83 YDS, 1 TD

RECEIVING YARDS
DEN	O. Daniels	6 REC, 102 YDS, 1 TD
IND	T.Y. Hilton	5 REC, 82 YDS

Broncos receiver Emmanuel Sanders (10) turns up field on his way to a 64-yard touchdown reception. *AP Photo*

Manning's 1-yard touchdown pass to tight end Owen Daniels, capping a nine-play, 80-yard drive. Manning completed a 27-yard pass to Daniels and a 17-yarder to wide receiver Demaryius Thomas during the drive. A pass-interference penalty against Colts cornerback Greg Toler in the end zone set up the scoring pass to Daniels.

But it was not enough.

"We were just out of whack," said Broncos safety T.J. Ward. "It wasn't the scheme that got us. It was assignment errors and penalties."

Denver pulled even at 17 with 4:57 left in the third quarter on kicker Brandon McManus's 29-yard field goal.

Manning's 37-yard pass to Daniels gave the Broncos a first down at the Colts' 18-yard line.

The Broncos got right back into the game on Manning's 64-yard touchdown pass to wide receiver Emmanuel Sanders on a third-and-14 play with 11:27 remaining in the third quarter, slicing the deficit to 17-14.

Backup free safety Omar Bolden returned a punt 83 yards for a touchdown on the first half's final play, injecting life into a Denver team that sputtered offensively throughout the first 30 minutes.

Bolden's return down the right sideline sliced the Colts' lead to 17-7.■

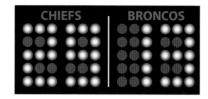

CHIEFS	BRONCOS

vs. Kansas City Chiefs, Nov. 15
Sports Authority Field at Mile High
Denver, Colorado

TURNOVER PRONE BRONCOS LOSE TO KC

A banged-up Peyton Manning was no match for the Kansas City Chiefs' relentless defense.

The Chiefs pressured Manning into a mistake-filled outing that included four interceptions and culminated in his third-quarter benching, and Kansas City shut down the Denver Broncos long enough for a 29-13 victory Sunday.

"Listen, defense, defense, defense," Chiefs coach Andy Reid said. "They did a tremendous job, five turnovers. They were able to put pressure on Peyton. That doesn't happen very often."

Charcandrick West ran for a touchdown and caught an 80-yard scoring pass from Alex Smith, helping the Chiefs (4-5) snap a seven-game losing streak to the Broncos (7-2). Cairo Santos added five field goals.

It was the second straight loss for the Broncos after opening the season with seven consecutive wins.

Though Manning became the NFL's all-time leading passer with his first completion of the day, he was also lifted from the game after playing ineffectively and struggling to dodge pressure while playing with sore ribs and a foot injury.

He finished 5 of 20 for 35 yards before being benched.

"I felt good enough to go out there and play," Manning said. "If you look back on it now, I have a hard time saying that's why I played badly. Could that be the reason? I guess it always could be. But to me, that's an easy way out."

Broncos coach Gary Kubiak said he made the decision to pull Manning because, "I was protecting him. ... I was worried about him."

Broncos receiver Demaryius Thomas (88) turns up field and picks up a block from teammate Bennie Fowler (16) on Chiefs defensive back Ron Parker (38). *AP Photo*

Kubiak also second-guessed himself for allowing Manning to play after the rib issue cropped up late in the week.

"I probably should have right there said, 'No, he's not going to go this week,' " Kubiak said. "But he's a competitor. He wanted to play."

Manning was replaced by backup Brock Osweiler with 6:34 left to play in the third quarter after throwing his fourth interception.

Kubiak said Manning remains the starter and he will start next week's game at Chicago if his health permits.

Osweiler led the Broncos on a drive that Ronnie Hillman finished with a 1-yard touchdown run with 5:27 left to play, averting the Broncos' first-ever shutout at home. The 2-point conversion try failed when a scrambling Osweiler was tackled short of the goal line.

However, Osweiler also had an interception in the end zone, by safety Eric Berry and the Chiefs capitalized on the turnover with Smith hitting West for the long catch-and-run touchdown early in the fourth quarter.

In all, the Chiefs scored 20 points off Denver's five turnovers.

Osweiler, who also had a 7-yard touchdown pass to Andre Caldwell in the late going, finished 14 of 24 for 146 yards.

Manning completed a 4-yard pass to Hillman during the first quarter of Sunday's game against Kansas City on Sunday to become the NFL's all-time passing yardage leader, surpassing the previous high by Brett Favre.

The completion boosted Manning's career yardage total to 71,840. Favre finished his career with 71,838.

The game was stopped momentarily to acknowledge Manning's feat. Hillman gave Manning the ball back for a keepsake and the quarterback tossed it to the Broncos sideline to have it put away.■

BOX SCORE

	1	2	3	4	T
Kansas City	10	9	3	7	29
Denver	0	0	0	13	13

GAME LEADERS

PASSING YARDS

| KC | A. Smith | 17-31, 204 YDS, 1 TD |
| DEN | B. Osweiler | 14-24, 146 YDS, 1 TD, 1 INT |

RUSHING YARDS

| KC | C. West | 24 CAR, 69 YDS, 1 TD |
| DEN | R. Hillman | 11 CAR, 42 YDS, 1 TD |

RECEIVING YARDS

| KC | C. West | 3 REC, 92 YDS, 1 TD |
| DEN | D. Thomas | 7 REC, 71 YDS |

Linebacker Brandon Marshall (54) and cornerback Chris Harris Jr (25) bring down Chiefs quarterback Alex Smith (11) after a short gain. *AP Photo*

Quarterback Brock Osweiler (17) attempts a quick pass intended for Andre Caldwell (12). Osweiler completed 20-27 passes for 250 yards on the day. *AP Photo*

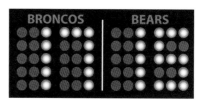

BRONCOS	BEARS

**at Chicago Bears, Nov. 22
Soldier Field
Chicago, Illinois**

OSWEILER LEADS BRONCOS PAST BEARS 17-15

The seeds of Denver's 17-15 victory Sunday over Chicago in quarterback Brock Osweiler's NFL starting debut apparently were planted a night earlier when the Broncos' charter plane spent two hours circling O'Hare before landing in a snowstorm.

Well, at least that was what several of them pointed to as a bonding moment for a team that had lost two straight games and was going on the road with its regular starting quarterback, Peyton Manning, sitting at home injured.

Coach Gary Kubiak even joked he might work a regular delay into the travel schedule. Better yet, if he can orchestrate a running game that produces 170 rushing yards (102 in 21 carries by Ronnie Hillman) and a young quarterback who can avoid any mistakes.

Osweiler, who has spent his entire four-year career as Manning's backup, completed 20 of 27 passes for 250 yards and two touchdowns and a passer rating of 127.1, a figure Manning, the future Hall of Famer, had not reached in exactly 52 weeks.

"Today is not about me," Osweiler said. "Today is 100 percent about this team and coaching staff. We played great defense, we didn't turn the ball over, and we ran the heck out of the football."

The only problem the 6-foot-8 Osweiler

Broncos running back Ronnie Hillman (23) powers through the line for a tough 7-yard gain during third quarter action.
AP Photo

had appeared to be avoiding a strong Chicago pass rush. He was sacked five times, compared to just 15 sacks of Manning in nine games. But Manning also had thrown 17 interceptions, and Osweiler threw none.

"The list of things I've learned behind Peyton is endless," Osweiler said. "I was comfortable. I really was, from the very first snap."

A fast start didn't hurt. Osweiler drove the Broncos 74 yards to a touchdown in four plays on their first possession, and the Bears never caught up. The touchdown was a 48-yard

pass play from Osweiler to Demaryius Thomas.

"Any time you can start the game like we did on the first drive is huge," Osweiler said.

The game was not decided, however, until only 24 seconds remained when the Bears, who failed to score a point on two excellent opportunities earlier in the fourth quarter, got a two-yard touchdown run from Jeremy Langford, who then was stopped attempting to run in for a two-point PAT.

Denver's victory ended a two-game losing streak and left the Broncos with an 8-2 record and still in strong contention for a

BOX SCORE

	1	2	3	4	T
Denver	7	3	0	7	17
Chicago	0	6	3	6	15

GAME LEADERS

PASSING YARDS
DEN	B. Osweiler	20-27, 250 YDS, 2 TD
CHI	J. Cutler	18-32, 265 YDS, 1 INT

RUSHING YARDS
DEN	R. Hillman	21 CAR, 102 YDS
CHI	K. Carey	9 CAR, 32 YDS

RECEIVING YARDS
DEN	O. Daniels	4 REC, 69 YDS
CHI	M. Wilson	4 REC, 102 YDS

Broncos cornerback Aqib Talib (21) defends on a pass intended for Bears running back Jeremy Langford (33). *AP Photo*

Quarterback Brock Osweiler addresses the team in the locker room after receiving a game ball for leading the Broncos to the win over the Bears. *AP Photo*

first-round playoff bye in the AFC. Chicago, which had won two in a row, dropped to 4-6 and now is only a game ahead of last-place Detroit in the NFC North.

Bears coach John Fox, who was fired as the Denver coach after the 2014 season, might have regrets over one of Chicago's failed four-quarter opportunities. With Denver ahead, 17-9 and 10 minutes remaining, the Bears had second-and-goal at the Broncos 4-yard line. Three straight passes by

Jay Cutler fell incomplete when a field goal on fourth down might have been the prudent call, considering the time remaining, since Chicago needed to score twice to win.

"You know, we hadn't made many trips down to the end zone," Fox said. "We hadn't scored touchdowns. It had been kind of a field goal game. At that point in the game, we felt that was going to be maybe our last opportunity. So we were aggressive and came up short."■

One of the knocks on DeMarcus Ware when he played for the Dallas Cowboys was that he rarely made the big plays at the big moments even if the statistics told otherwise.

In the Denver Broncos' divisional round win against the Pittsburgh Steelers, Ware made two of the biggest plays of the game. He recovered a fumble that the Broncos turned into the go-ahead touchdown and recorded a fourth-down sack that put the game away. In 47 snaps, Ware had three tackles, two tackles for loss, a quarterback hurry in addition to the sack and fumble recovery.

On the fumble recovery, Ware said he made a mistake in reading pass at the snap, giving Fitzgerald Toussaint room on a delayed run. He spun back and was able to dive on the fumble created by Bradley Roby.

On the sack of Ben Roethlisberger, he slid underneath going right to left and found the Steelers' quarterback in his view after Von Miller got the initial pressure.

The Cowboys released Ware after the 2013 season after he recorded six sacks and missed the first three games of his career. He also had a bloated salary cap figure that the team created by continuously restructuring his contract over the years.

The Cowboys never made an offer to keep Ware and the Broncos offered him something he could not refuse: $20 million guaranteed on a three-year, $30 million contract. In 27 games with the Broncos Ware has recorded 17.5 sacks and formed one of the best pass-rushing duos with Miller.

This year he was reunited with Wade Phillips and had 4.5 sacks in the first four games before a back strain slowed him down.

Since Ware's departure, the Cowboys' leaders in sacks have been Jeremy Mincey (six in 2014) and DeMarcus Lawrence (eight in 2015). Ware arrived to the Cowboys with an innate ability to get to the quarterback and he left as the franchise's all-time leader in sacks with 117.

And he hasn't lost that ability in Denver.

With the big plays coming at the most opportune times, Ware finds himself paying in his first Super Bowl appearance of his career.

In 2007 and 2009 with the Cowboys and then last year with the Broncos, Ware suffered through divisional round losses to the New York Giants, Minnesota Vikings and Indianapolis Colts. "For me, I've played in playoff games three times and never sort of been able to close it out," Ware said. "So this right here is that chapter where you can write it down and say you did that, but for me it's always, 'What have you done for me lately?' I'm still writing on that page and trying to get to the end. We'll be ready for Carolina and I'm excited about it." ■

GAME ELEVEN

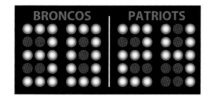

BRONCOS   PATRIOTS

**vs. New England Patriots, Nov. 29
Sports Authority Field at Mile High
Denver, Colorado**

BRONCOS RALLY TO BEAT PATRIOTS IN OT

Recognizing the run play that was called likely would go nowhere against the New England Patriots' defensive alignment, Denver Broncos quarterback Brock Osweiler audibled to a different one. The result was electric.

Running back C.J. Anderson broke loose through the snow for a game-winning, 48-yard touchdown run, and the Broncos rallied to beat New England 30-24 in overtime Sunday night, handing the Patriots their first loss of the season.

"The run that we had called was no good," Osweiler said. "I just checked to the second play. It was a check we had worked on in practice all week. Our line did a hell of a job, and C.J. did the rest."

Denver's defense set up the Broncos' final drive by stopping quarterback Tom Brady and the Patriots (10-1) on the first possession of overtime.

Anderson shook free from a couple of Patriots defenders en route to the decisive score.

"We needed a big play to try to bring this game home," said Denver wide receiver Andre Caldwell, who caught a key touchdown pass from Osweiler in the final minutes of regulation.

54

Patriots quarterback Tom Brady is brought down by the Broncos Shane Ray (56) and Malik Jackson (97). *AP Photo*

"When I saw him in the open field, I knew he was gone. And the fans went crazy. That was the wildest I've seen this place in a long time."

Osweiler, making his second career start in place of injured Peyton Manning, was 23 of 42 for 270 yards with a touchdown pass. He was intercepted once.

Brady completed 23 of 42 for 280 yards, connecting with running back Brandon Bolden and tight ends Scott Chandler and Rob Gronkowski for touchdowns. Gronkowski (six catches, 88 yards) took a hard hit trying to make a catch with just under three minutes remaining and was carted off the field with a knee injury.

"We'll keep fighting," Brady said. "We lost tonight, it was tough game, come on the road, we had a good lead. We just didn't make a couple of plays in the fourth quarter. We had plenty of opportunities to win."

Osweiler gave Denver (9-2) its first lead of the night, 24-21, when he completed a 4-yard touchdown pass to Caldwell with 1:09 remaining in regulation.

That was enough time for Brady to drive the Patriots to Denver 29-yard line. As time expired, kicker Stephen Gostkowski drilled a 47-yard field amidst the snow flurries to send the game into overtime.

New England appeared to gain control of the game when Brady lofted a pass downfield to Bolden, who slipped past a tackler at about the 30 to turn it into a 63-yard catch and run for a touchdown on the first play of the fourth quarter. The Patriots led 21-7.

A special teams mistake got Denver back in the game.

Chris Harper fumbled a punt, and Broncos linebacker Shaquil Barrett recovered at the New England 36. That led to Anderson's

Broncos receiver Andre Caldwell (12) keeps his feet in bounds for a 4-yard touchdown reception giving Denver a 24-21 lead late in the fourth quarter. *AP Photo*

57

15-yard touchdown run, which pulled Denver within 21-14 with 12:34 remaining. Anderson finished with 15 carries for 113 yards and two touchdowns.

Osweiler drove the Broncos to the Patriots' 3-yard line, but after a third-down pass fell incomplete in the end zone, Brandon McManus came on to kick a 21-yard field goal with 6:12 to play, setting the stage for a frenetic finish.

Denver wide receiver Emmanuel Sanders had six receptions for 113 yards.

The Broncos fell behind 14-0 before they put together a long drive that running back Ronnie Hillman finished with a 19-yard touchdown run to pull within seven at the half. Osweiler kept the drive alive with a 3-yard sneak on a fourth-and-1 play. ∎

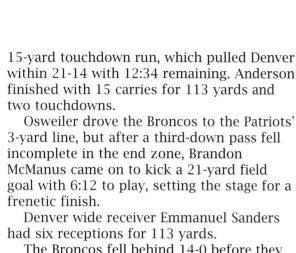

▶Broncos running back C.J. Anderson (22) races 48 yards for the game-winning touchdown. *AP Photo*

▼Quarterback Brock Osweiler gives C.J. Anderson a hug following Anderson's game-winning 48-yard touchdown run. *AP Photo*

BOX SCORE

	1	2	3	4	OT	T
New England	7	7	0	10	0	24
Denver	0	7	0	17	6	30

GAME LEADERS

PASSING YARDS
NE	T. Brady	23-42, 280 YDS, 3 TD
DEN	B. Osweiler	23-42, 270 YDS, 1 TD, 1 INT

RUSHING YARDS
NE	L. Blount	9 CAR, 27 YDS
DEN	C.J. Anderson	15 CAR, 113 YDS, 2 TD

RECEIVING YARDS
NE	R. Gronkowski	6 REC, 88 YDS, 1 TD
DEN	E. Sanders	6 REC, 113 YDS

GAME TWELVE

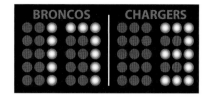

at San Diego Chargers, Dec. 6
Qaulcomm Stadium
San Diego, California

BRONCOS BREEZE PAST CHARGERS 17-3

Those predicting the Denver Broncos' demise when Peyton Manning got hurt are having second thoughts.

Brock Osweiler improved to 3-0 and Denver breezed past the San Diego Chargers 17-3 on Sunday at Qualcomm Stadium.

With the win, the 10-2 Broncos tightened their grip on first place in the AFC West and kept pace with the AFC-leading Cincinnati Bengals in the conference in the race for home-field advantage in the postseason.

What's been uprooted is the notion the Broncos would collapse without Manning, the five-time NFL MVP.

"No one blinked with this being a road game," Osweiler said. "We got a quick start, a quick score and then we slowed down a bit throughout the game. We did what we had to do to stay into it."

Osweiler completed 16 of 26 passes for a touchdown and 166 yards. He was intercepted once.

"I think he continues to grow," Denver coach Gary Kubiak. "The thing I really liked about him was he learns from his mistakes."

The Broncos raced to a 17-0 second-quarter lead and coasted in for the win.

For the dreadful Chargers (3-9), the loss was their fifth straight home defeat and fifth in a row against the AFC West.

"Obviously not too many bright spots," said Chargers coach Mike McCoy said.

Broncos receiver Demaryius Thomas (88) slips the tackle of San Diego cornerback Patrick Robinson (26). *AP Photo*

Quarterback Philip Rivers was 18 of 35 for 202 yards. He had an interception returned for a touchdown and San Diego turned it over three times.

Rivers was sacked four times and the Chargers failed to score a touchdown for the second game in a row.

The constant in the win streak has been the Broncos' top-ranked defense.

"They've got a lot of guys who can rush," Rivers said. "At times we moved the ball and got into their territory. We couldn't finish drives and then we had the turnovers. That's a

BOX SCORE

	1	2	3	4	T
Denver	14	3	0	0	17
San Diego	0	3	0	0	3

GAME LEADERS

PASSING YARDS
DEN	B. Osweiler	16-26, 166 YDS, 1 TD, 1 INT
SD	P. Rivers	18-35, 202 YDS, 1 INT

RUSHING YARDS
DEN	R. Hillman	19 CAR, 56 YDS
SD	M. Gordon	12 CAR, 55 YDS

RECEIVING YARDS
DEN	D. Thomas	6 REC, 61 YDS, 1 TD
SD	A. Gates	6 REC, 50 YDS

heck of a group and we didn't rise to the challenge."

Late in the first half, Josh Lambo's 51-yard field goal sliced the Chargers' deficit to 17-3. Lambo was wide right on a 48-yard attempt earlier in the second quarter.

Denver's Brandon McManus was true on his 23-yard attempt, stretching the Broncos' advantage to 17-0

The Broncos increased their lead to 14-0 in the first-quarter's waning seconds.

Rivers, under duress, delivered his pass early and linebacker Danny Trevathan broke to the ball. He brought it back 25 yards for a touchdown, the fifth pick-6 Rivers has thrown this season and the fifth defensive touchdown on the season for Denver.

Osweiler's 3-yard touchdown pass to wide receiver Demaryius Thomas capped a 76-yard opening drive.

"The main thing was to start fast," Thomas said.

Thomas finished with a game-high 61 yards on six receptions. Each catch was greeted with a roar, as Broncos fans filled Qualcomm Stadium.

"We've gotten used to it, unfortunately," a resigned Rivers said.

Not Osweiler.

"Oh my god, it was unbelievable how much orange," he said. "It's just a testament that we truly have the best fans in the world."

"When the defense was on the field, it was loud," Thomas said about the crowd. "I was not used to that. It was good for us." ∎

Denver defensive coordinator Wade Phillips and linebacker Von Miller (left) celebrate after Phillips received a game ball for the Broncos defensive effort. *AP Photo*

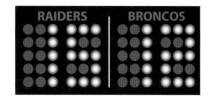

vs. Oakland Raiders, Dec. 13
Sports Authority Field at Mile High
Denver, Colorado

BRONCOS CAN'T HANG ON IN LOSS TO RAIDERS

The Denver Broncos couldn't hold on to Brock Osweiler's passes or hold off Khalil Mack's pass rushes.

Mack had five second-half sacks, including one in the end zone for a safety, and Derek Carr bounced back from an awful first half to lead the Oakland Raiders past Denver 15-12 Sunday.

Carr completed just 12 of 29 passes for 135 yards. But two of his throws were for touchdowns, and the Raiders (6-7) beat the Broncos for the first time since Sept. 12, 2011 despite being held to minus-12 yards in the first half -- the worst performance by a team heading into halftime in nearly a quarter-century.

The Broncos (10-3) began the game as the AFC's top seed but couldn't finish drives, hold onto a 12-0 halftime lead or onto several on-target throws from Osweiler. Demaryius Thomas had two big drops, one for a touchdown and another for a late first down. He also lost a fumble.

The one that really stung was a drop by a wide-open Vernon Davis at the Oakland 42 on fourth-and-5 from the Denver 37 with 3:45 left.

"I got super excited because I knew I was going to be wide open, took my eyes off the ball and wasn't able to pull it in," Davis said.

Osweiler refused to blame his receivers for their many mistakes, his coaches for a conservative game plan, his running backs for gaining just 1.6 yards a carry, or his protection for getting him clobbered.

Denver quarterback Brock Osweiler (17) attempts to scramble away from Raiders defensive end Khalil Mack (52). *AP Photo*

Quarterback Brock Osweiler (17) completes one of his 51 pass attempts as Oakland defensive tackle Dan Williams (90) applies pressure. *AP Photo*

"No reason to point any fingers," said Osweiler, who completed 35 of 51 passes for 308 yards.

Mack's fifth sack helped snuff out Denver's final drive. Mack said the Raiders knew they had a chance when they held the Broncos out of the end zone four times in the first half.

The Raiders drove 80 yards to open the second half and trim Denver's lead to 12-7 when Carr threw an 11-yard pass to Seth Roberts. A safety pulled the Raiders to 12-9 when Mack sacked Osweiler in the end zone and Broncos guard Max Garcia recovered the loose ball.

"He was unbelievable," Raiders coach Jack Del Rio said of Mack. "He's just getting better and better."

Oakland long snapper Jon Condo recovered Emmanuel Sanders' muffed punt at the Denver 11 early in the fourth quarter, but he injured his right shoulder in the pile. He was in the locker room getting it looked at when Carr threw a 16-yard touchdown pass to tight end Mychal Rivera to put Oakland ahead 15-12 with 14:26 remaining.

Without Condo, the Raiders went for 2 and Carr threw an incompletion, leaving the margin at a field goal.

Brandon McManus clanked a 49-yarder that would have tied it off the left upright with 10:22 remaining. Sebastian Janikowski then missed a 43-yarder with 5:07 remaining, giving the Broncos good field position at their 33, but Davis had his big drop on fourth down after that.

The Broncos couldn't get into the end zone in the first half despite 224 yards of offense, settling for four field goals from McManus, each one shorter than the previous — 41, 35, 29 and 21 yards.

"We had a chance to really do some damage in the first half and didn't do it," Denver coach Gary Kubiak lamented. "And we obviously helped them in the second half with turnovers, I think four or five drops." ■

BOX SCORE

	1	2	3	4	T
Oakland	0	0	9	6	15
Denver	6	6	0	0	12

GAME LEADERS

PASSING YARDS

OAK	D. Carr	12-29, 135 YDS, 2 TD	
DEN	B. Osweiler	35-51, 308 YDS	

RUSHING YARDS

OAK	L. Murray	16 CAR, 27 YDS
DEN	R. Hillman	12 CAR, 20 YDS

RECEIVING YARDS

OAK	M. Rivera	3 REC, 49 YDS, 1 TD
DEN	D. Thomas	10 REC, 95 YDS

Broncos defenders Derek Wolfe (95) and Todd Davis (51) stop Raiders fullback Marcel Reece (45) for no gain during fourth quarter action. *AP Photo*

Denver receiver Emmanuel Sanders (10) blows past Pittsburgh free safety Mike Mitchell (23) for a 61-yard touchdown reception. *AP Photo*

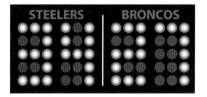

STEELERS | BRONCOS

at Pittsburgh Steelers, Dec. 20
Heinz Field
Pittsburgh, Pennsylvania

STEELERS RALLY FOR 34-27 WIN

Quarterback Ben Roethlisberger threw for 380 yards and three touchdowns — including a game-winning 23-yard strike to wide receiver Antonio Brown with 3:24 remaining - as the Pittsburgh Steelers rallied from a 17-point deficit to beat the Denver Broncos 34-27 at Heinz Field.

Roethlisberger's second touchdown pass to Brown, who had 16 receptions for 189 yards, broke a 27-27 tie and gave the Steelers (9-5) their fifth win in six games. The score came three plays after Steelers linebacker Ryan Shazier intercepted Brock Osweiler at the Broncos' 37-yard line.

Roethlisberger completed 40 of 55 passes against the NFL's No. 1 defense in points (17.3 per game) and total yards (272.3) allowed. The Broncos had two interceptions, including a pick by linebacker Brandon Marshall with 2:08 left at the Steelers' 41.

The Broncos were unable to take advantage of the turnover as Osweiler threw four straight incomplete passes, giving the ball back to the Steelers on downs with 1:40 remaining.

Pittsburgh ran out the clock.

Steelers wide receiver Martavis Bryant added 10 receptions for 87 yards.

"They made plays in big situations," Broncos cornerback Aqib Talib said. "We needed to tackle better. Kudos to those boys."

Osweiler, threw three touchdowns passes

Broncos cornerback Bradley Roby (29) looks to make the tackle on Steelers receiver Antonio Brown (84). *AP Photo*

and ran for another as the Broncos built a 27-10 lead in the second quarter.

However, Denver (10-4) failed to score in the second half and lost a second straight game to see its lead in the AFC West over the Chiefs trimmed to one game. The Broncos have been shut out in the second half of each of their last three games.

"I think there were some plays we should have made by a lot of people, not just the quarterback," Broncos coach Gary Kubiak said. "I think we executed really well in the first half. I just don't think we executed the same way in the second half."

Osweiler was 21 of 44 passing for 296 yards and was intercepted once. In the second half, though, he was 7 of 26 for 82 yards. He injured his left - non-throwing - shoulder late in the second quarter and was briefly replaced by rookie quarterback Trevor Siemian before returning to the game.

BOX SCORE

	1	2	3	4	T
Denver	14	13	0	0	27
Pittsburgh	7	6	7	14	34

GAME LEADERS

PASSING YARDS
DEN B. Osweiler   21-44, 296 YDS, 3 TD, 1 INT
PIT   B. Roethlisberger   40-55, 380 YDS, 3 TD, 2 INT

RUSHING YARDS
DEN   R. Hillman   14 CAR, 48 YDS
PIT   D. Williams   14 CAR, 26 YDS, 1 TD

RECEIVING YARDS
DEN   E. Sanders   10 REC, 181 YDS, 1 TD
PIT   A. Brown   16 REC, 189 YDS, 2 TD

Former Steelers receiver Emmanuel Sanders had 10 receptions for 181 yards and a touchdown for the Broncos, but nine of the catches came in the first half for 139 yards. Wide receiver Demaryius Thomas had two touchdown catches.

The Steelers started their comeback on kicker Josh Boswell's 41-yard field goal with four seconds to go in the first half.

The Steelers tied it on a pair of 9-yard touchdown passes from Roethlisberger in the second half. He connected with Brown with 7:16 left in the third quarter and wide receiver Markus Wheaton with 12:34 remaining in the fourth period.

Osweiler tied the score with an 18-yard touchdown pass to Thomas with 4:45 left in the first quarter. A little less than 90 seconds later,

Sanders got behind the defense, which was blitzing Osweiler, and hauled in a 61-yard scoring pass to put the Broncos ahead 14-7.

Osweiler then ran 7 yards for a touchdown on third-and-goal to give the Broncos a two-touchdown lead with 11 1/2 minutes remaining in the second quarter. Kicker Brandon McManus missed the extra-point attempt at the end of the 10-play drive.

After a 24-yard field goal by Boswell, Osweiler and Thomas connected on a 6-yard score with 1:50 to go in the second quarter to put the Broncos up 27-10. ∎

Broncos quarterback Brock Osweiler (17) sprints past Steelers strong safety Will Allen (20) for a 7-yard touchdown run. *AP Photo*

Denver linebacker DeMarcus Ware (94) moves into position to recover a fumble by Cincinnati quarterback AJ McCarron (5). The fumble recovery by Ware secured the overtime win for the Broncos. *AP Photo*

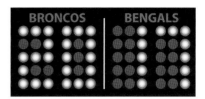

vs. Cincinnati Bengals, Dec. 28
Sports Authority Field at Mile High
Denver, Colorado

BRONCOS CLINCH PLAYOFF BERTH WITH OT WIN

Linebacker DeMarcus Ware had the final say in the victory that clinched a playoff berth for the Denver Broncos.

Brandon McManus kicked a 37-yard field goal in overtime after missing one with no time left in regulation, Ware recovered a fumbled shotgun snap to prevent an answer from the Bengals, and the Broncos beat Cincinnati 20-17 Monday night.

"The ball was on the ground, and I was feeling like, 'There's no way somebody's going to take this ball from me,'" Ware said. "It felt great to finish the game that way. We thought we were going to finish it with the field goal at the end (of regulation), but it's all about that win."

Quarterback Brock Osweiler threw for a touchdown and led the overtime drive ending in McManus' game-winning field goal, helping the Broncos (11-4) clinch a playoff berth for a fifth consecutive season.

Running back C.J. Anderson added a 39-yard touchdown run for Denver, which can lock up the AFC West title with a win over the San Diego Chargers in the regular-season finale at home on Sunday.

"We wanted to put ourselves in the playoffs, and we still control things we want to control moving on to San Diego," Anderson said.

The Broncos' defense sealed the victory

when a snap went through the arms of Cincinnati quarterback AJ McCarron. Ware recovered the fumble, ending the overtime possession for the Bengals (11-4), who also are playoff-bound.

"It was my fault," said McCarron, who injured his left wrist diving for the loose ball. "I looked up to see the coverage, and the snap caught me by surprise."

Denver had a chance to win the game at the end of the fourth quarter, but McManus shanked a 45-yard field-goal try wide left.

Osweiler finished 27 of 39 for 299 yards with one touchdown pass and no interceptions. McCarron completed 22 of 35 for 200 yards with one scoring pass and no interceptions.

Trailing by 11, the Broncos aired it out to open the third quarter, marching 81 yards largely on the strength of Osweiler's passing arm. He finished off the drive with an 8-yard pass to wide receiver Emmanuel Sanders, who broke through cornerback Adam Jones' tackle near the goal line for Denver's first touchdown of the game with 10:14 left in the period.

It was Denver's first second-half score in four games, and it would not be the team's last, though the Broncos turned to their running game.

After the Broncos' forced a

Broncos receiver Emmanuel Sanders (10) sneaks in to score as Bengals cornerback Adam Jones (24) defends. *AP Photo*

BOX SCORE

	1	2	3	4	OT	T
Cincinnati	7	7	0	3	0	17
Denver	0	3	7	7	3	20

GAME LEADERS

PASSING YARDS
CIN A. McCarron 22-35, 200 YDS, 1 TD
DEN B. Osweiler 27-39, 299 YDS, 1 TD

RUSHING YARDS
CIN J. Hill 19 CAR, 63 YDS
DEN C.J. Anderson 9 CAR, 73 YDS, 1 TD

RECEIVING YARDS
CIN A.J. Green 5 REC, 57 YDS, 1 TD
DEN O. Daniels 5 REC, 70 YDS

Broncos running back C.J. Anderson breaks free on a 39-yard touchdown run as Bengals free safety Reggie Nelson (20) and cornerback Adam Jones (24) defend. *AP Photo*

Broncos kicker Brandon McManus (8) watches his overtime field goal split the uprights. *AP Photo*

punt, Denver took over on its 48. Osweiler passed 13 yards to wide receiver Demaryius Thomas and before handing off to Anderson. With the middle clogged, Anderson darted to his left, broke the tackle of defensive end Wallace Gilberry near the line of scrimmage and sprinted 39 yards down the left sideline, eluding two more tackles before going in for the score to put Denver up by three with 11:17 remaining.

Cincinnati evened the score on kicker Mike Nugent's 52-yard field goal with 6:46 left to play.

The Bengals stopped Denver's subsequent drive when they forced Anderson to fumble at the Cincinnati 26-yard line with about four minutes left. It was recovered by Bengals safety Reggie Nelson.

However, the Broncos' defense again forced a punt.

"There's an old saying: 'It's not how you start, it's how you finish,'" Broncos quarterback Brock Osweiler said. "And this team finished great tonight."■

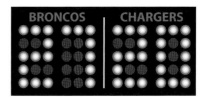

vs. San Diego Chargers, Jan. 3
Sports Authority Field at Mile High
Denver, Colorado

MANNING LEADS BRONCOS PAST CHARGERS

Quarterback Peyton Manning helped turn Coach Gary Kubiak's gut feeling into a winning move.

Cast in the unfamiliar role of backup, Manning came off the bench to relieve an ineffective Brock Osweiler and led four second-half scoring drives, and the Denver Broncos rallied to beat to the San Diego Chargers 27-20 on Sunday. The victory clinched the AFC West title and the conference's No. 1 playoff seed.

"It's been a different year certainly, a different week, different approach," Manning said. "I think when I was in there, we ran the ball better. We held on to the ball, caught the ball better. That's just kind of how it worked out."

Relying more on his leadership and steadying influence than his passing arm in his first action in seven weeks, Manning drove the Broncos (12-4) to a pair of field goals by kicker Brandon McManus and on marches that ended in touchdown runs by C.J. Anderson and Ronnie Hillman.

"He told us to go out and put some points on the board and that's what we did," wide receiver Demaryius Thomas said of Manning. "He told everyone to calm down. He came in and was the leader that he is."

Broncos receiver Demaryius Thomas (88) avoids defenders on his way to the end zone for a 72-yard touchdown reception.
AP Photo

Denver safety Shiloh Keo (33) is congratulated by teammates Derek Wolfe (95) and Malik Jackson after making an interception. *AP Photo*

Hillman finished with 117 rushing yards, including a tiebreaking 23-yard touchdown run with 4:44 left to play on the first play after safety Shiloh Keo's interception of a pass from quarterback Philip Rivers.

The Broncos, defense stopped San Diego's final possession on downs, and Manning took a knee to run out the final few seconds.

Kubiak said he decided to go with Manning after the Broncos were set back by their fifth turnover of the game during the third quarter.

"Just my gut told me to turn it over to him," Kubiak said. "I'm just very proud of him. He's worked really hard to stay there for us and it couldn't be a bigger day to be there for us."

Coupled with the New England Patriots' loss earlier to the Miami Dolphins, the Broncos claimed the top seed and a first-round playoff bye in addition to their fifth consecutive division crown.

"It lifted the whole stadium," Broncos cornerback Aqib Talib said of Manning's insertion into the game. "It lifted the O-line. The O-line got with it and we opened up some holes and got to running that ball. I don't know if it as just his

presence, but it was just a little energy that came through the building."

Greeted by roaring crowd, Manning led a drive that leaned on the running of Anderson with a couple of key completions along the way. Anderson's 1-yard scoring run with 5:24 left in the third gave Denver a 14-13 lead.

McManus added a 48-yard field goal for Denver before the Chargers (4-12) regained the lead on Philip Rivers' 80-yard scoring pass to Tyrell Williams, who somehow was all alone downfield for the long-

BOX SCORE

	1	2	3	4	T
San Diego	3	3	7	7	20
Denver	7	0	7	13	27

GAME LEADERS

PASSING YARDS

SD	P. Rivers	21-35, 228 YDS, 2 TD, 1 INT
DEN	B. Osweiler	14-22, 232 YDS, 1 TD, 2 INT

RUSHING YARDS

SD	D. Brown	21 CAR, 81 YDS
DEN	R. Hillman	15 CAR, 117 YDS, 1 TD

RECEIVING YARDS

SD	T. Williams	2 REC, 90 YDS, 1 TD
DEN	D. Thomas	5 REC, 117 YDS, 1 TD

distance touchdown that put San Diego back on top 20-17 with 12:58 to play.

Again, Manning led the Broncos to a score, as McManus' 35-yarder capped a 63-yard drive and tied the game 20-20 with 9:48 to go.

Manning finished 5-for-9 for 69 yards Sunday. Osweiler was 14-for-22 for 232 yards with one touchdown pass and two interceptions.

The Broncos dominated play in the first half but clung to a 7-6 lead at halftime. Denver committed four first-half turnovers, including three by Osweiler on a pair of interceptions and a fumble after a sack.∎

Denver Broncos quarterback Peyton Manning has experienced the Super Bowl as a winner and loser.

He was the MVP of a victory over Chicago in Super Bowl XLI. He threw an interception that was returned for a touchdown in each of his Super Bowl losses, to New Orleans in Super Bowl XLIV and to Seattle in Super Bowl XLVIII.

Given that Super Bowl 50 will be his fourth trip to the league's title game, Manning is the Broncos' most experienced player, not only in total years in the league (18) but, in dealing with the circus that surrounds the big game.

Manning said he has taken more from winning than he has from losing.

"I can't say there are a lot of positives in going through a Super Bowl loss," Manning said. "It's not a fun experience. Does it fuel you? Yeah. I think it depends on who you are and kind of what drives you. But when you play in the NFL, it's driven me every year to try to be a better player than I was the year before and to try and do my best for the team. That's kind of the case this year. I'm very grateful for the opportunity to be going back to a Super Bowl, and I can certainly attest that winning is a lot better than losing."

If experience does indeed matter in Super Bowl 50, the Broncos have a large advantage over the Carolina Panthers, starting with Manning.

The five-time league MVP has completed 68 percent of his passes in three previous Super Bowl trips, with three touchdowns and four interceptions. At 39 years old, he will be the oldest quarterback to start a Super Bowl.

Overall, the Broncos have 18 players who have played in a Super Bowl, 16 of whom were with the Broncos for the team's 43-8 loss to Seattle in Super Bowl XLVIII. The Broncos have four other players — linebacker Von Miller, cornerback Chris Harris Jr., defensive end Derek Wolfe and linebacker Lerentee McCray — who were on injured reserve when the Broncos advanced to the title game against the Seahawks.

Perhaps a championship résumé gets a team through the week before the Super Bowl, but once the ball is kicked and flashes light up the stadium, Manning believes it's about what happens in the present, not the past.

"I still think it comes down to the preparation during the couple weeks, and it still comes down to the actual play on the field on the actual Sunday," Manning said. "I can't say that [experience] helps or hurts one way or the other.

"I know we've got a number of players who've been in a couple. We've got a lot of players going for their first time. I was visiting with [linebacker] Shane Ray and [cornerback] Taurean Nixon the other day, and I said, 'I wish I would've gone to a Super Bowl my rookie year.' We won three games that year. We were done in November. It was over. These guys that have been here three years, it's their second [Super Bowl] in three years.

"I try to remind them that's not the norm, and don't take it for granted." ▪

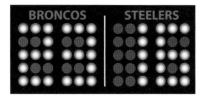

vs. Pittsburgh Steelers, Jan. 17
Sports Authority Field at Mile High
Denver, Colorado

BRONCOS ADVANCE TO AFC CHAMPIONSHIP GAME

Through the misfires, miscues and dropped passes, Peyton Manning stayed the course until it finally all came together for the Denver Broncos.

The veteran quarterback led a go-ahead touchdown drive in the fourth quarter following a Pittsburgh turnover, and the Broncos overcame some serious mistakes to beat the Steelers 23-16 Sunday and advance to the AFC title game for the second time in three years.

The Broncos, who also got five field goals from kicker Brandon McManus, will host Tom Brady and the New England Patriots in the AFC Championship Game on Jan. 24.

"One thing I've always believed in -- you have missed throws. You have some dropped passes. You just keep firing," said Manning, whose offense was stalled for much of the game by as many as eight drops by his receivers as well as some errant throws and penalties.

"We stayed patient tonight," Manning added. "We never really got frustrated, and it served us well tonight and it served me well this season."

Manning, making his first start since playing ineffectively in a Week 10 loss to the Kansas City Chiefs while fighting a foot injury, finally put together a sustained drive after Broncos cornerback Bradley Roby punched the ball from the grasp of running back Fitzgerald Toussaint. Denver linebacker DeMarcus Ware recovered the fumble at the

Denver quarterback Peyton Manning (18) throws downfield during first half action against Pittsburgh. *AP Photo*

Broncos 35-yard line with 9:52 left to play.

"Bottom line is when you lose a turnover battle in a hostile environment versus good people, it's going to cost you," Steelers coach Mike Tomlin said. "It cost us today."

The Steelers' defense nearly bailed Pittsburgh out, forcing the Broncos into a third-and-12 situation. However, Manning then hit the biggest pass of the game, connecting with wide receiver Bennie Fowler on a 31-yard completion to the Pittsburgh 36. Fowler had two critical drops earlier in the game before securing the catch that paved the way for a bruising finish to Denver's decisive drive.

"You could see, once I got the fumble and we got the turnover, Peyton went down and (the offense) scored," Ware said. "The momentum built from there, and we were able to close the game out."

Denver running backs Ronnie Hillman and C.J. Anderson alternated on key runs to move the chains before Anderson broke through for a touchdown from 1-yard out with three minutes

remaining.

Manning, who led his 55th career game-winning drive in the fourth-quarter or overtime and second in his playoff career, then passed to wide receiver Demaryius Thomas for the two-point conversion and a seven-point Denver advantage.

Manning completed 21 of 37 passes for 222 yards on the day.

After Denver held Pittsburgh, forcing the ball back to the Broncos on downs, McManus kicked a 45-yard field goal with 53 seconds to play to make it a two-score lead.

The Steelers managed a 49-yard field goal by kicker Chris Boswell with 19 seconds left, but Anderson recovered the Steelers' onside kick, and Manning took a knee to run out the last few seconds.

"It's tough," Steelers quarterback Ben Roethlisberger said. "It's emotional for everybody because everybody appreciates everybody else's effort. Only one team ends the season the way they want to."

Roethlisberger, playing through a shoulder

Broncos cornerback Bradley Roby, right, forces a key fourth-quarter fumble by Steelers running back Fitzgerald Toussaint that was recovered by teammate DeMarcus Ware at the Broncos 35-yard line. *AP Photo*

Broncos running back C.J. Anderson (22) lunges into the end zone for a 1-yard touchdown with 3:04 remaining in the fourth quarter. *AP Photo*

injury, completed 24 of 37 passes and with 339 yards, topping 300 yards for the second time this season against the Broncos. No other quarterback reached 300 against Denver this season.

"They're a big-play football team," Broncos coach Gary Kubiak said. "But the good news is that we settled down defensively and found a way to sit there and hold them to 16 points."

McManus' fourth field goal, a 41-yarder with 2:45 remaining in the third quarter, pulled the Broncos to within a point. Denver's drive stalled in part when linebacker James Harrison set back the Broncos with a sack of Manning.

Earlier in the third, the Steelers got a 28-yard field goal from Boswell.

Plagued by eight drops in the first half, the Broncos were limited to three field goals by McManus. He kicked a 51-yarder through swirling winds as time expired in the second quarter, and Denver trailed 10-9 at halftime.

Now the attention turns to Manning vs Brady one more time. Manning and Brady have squared off 16 times before, a full season's worth of matchups between the two quarterbacks whose careers are so intertwined.

Brady has won 11 of the 16 meetings against Manning, but they're 2-2 in the playoffs, including Denver's 26-16 win in the conference

Kicker Brandon McManus drills a 45-yard field goal to give the Broncos a 23-13 lead late in the fourth quarter. It was one of five field goals McManus made on the day. *AP Photo*

championship game two years ago.

"It'll be the Broncos vs. the Patriots," Manning said of the AFC's top two seeds, both 13-4. "We'll enjoy this one tonight. To kind of quote Bill Belichick, we'll be on to New England. I'll start talking about them on Wednesday." ∎

BOX SCORE

	1	2	3	4	T
Pittsburgh	7	3	3	3	16
Denver	6	3	3	11	23

SCORING SUMMARY

FIRST QUARTER
DEN FG 11:21 Brandon McManus 28 Yd Field Goal
Drive info: 5 plays, 20 yards, 1:57

DEN FG 3:40 Brandon McManus 41 Yd Field Goal
Drive info: 4 plays, 8 yards, 1:26

PIT TD 1:22 Fitzgerald Toussaint 1 Yd Run (Chris Boswell Kick)
Drive info: 5 plays, 80 yards, 2:18

SECOND QUARTER
PIT FG 10:19 Chris Boswell 43 Yd Field Goal
Drive info: 7 plays, 60 yards, 3:53

DEN FG 0:00 Brandon McManus 51 Yd Field Goal
Drive info: 11 plays, 62 yards, 3:14

THIRD QUARTER
PIT FG 9:32 Chris Boswell 28 Yd Field Goal
Drive info: 8 plays, 69 yards, 2:19

DEN FG 2:45 Brandon McManus 41 Yd Field Goal
Drive info: 7 plays, 30 yards, 3:08

FOURTH QUARTER
DEN TD 3:00 C.J. Anderson 1 Yd Run (Peyton Manning Pass to Demaryius Thomas for Two-Point Conversion)
Drive info: 6 plays, 61 yards, 2:15

DEN FG 0:53 Brandon McManus 45 Yd Field Goal
Drive info: 4 plays, 3 yards, 0:56

PIT FG 0:19 Chris Boswell 47 Yd Field Goal
Drive info: 4 plays, 51 yards, 0:34

GAME LEADERS

PASSING YARDS
PIT B. Roethlisberger 24-37, 339 YDS
DEN P. Manning 21-37, 222 YDS

RUSHING YARDS
PIT M. Bryant 2 CAR, 40 YDS
DEN C.J. Anderson 15 CAR, 72 YDS, 1 TD

RECEIVING YARDS
PIT M. Bryant 9 REC, 154 YDS
DEN E. Sanders 5 REC, 85 YDS

Broncos cornerback Aqib Talib (21) breaks up a pass intended for Steelers receiver Markus Wheaton (11). *AP Photo*

Pittsburgh quarterback Ben Roethlisberger is sacked by Broncos linebacker DeMarcus Ware. *AP Photo*

BRONCOS FEATURE

"I don't think you'll find a single player inside football that doesn't like Gary Kubiak. Even guys he cuts. He lets players do their thing."

— Houston Texans All-Pro defensive end J.J. Watt

John Elway and Gary Kubiak go back a few years. 33 to be exact.

Elway does not remember the first time he met Kubiak when they became Denver Broncos teammates in 1983, Kubiak an anonymous eighth-round draft choice, Elway the highly acclaimed No. 1 overall selection.

But Elway remembers the first time he was around Kubiak at their first minicamp in May of 1983, which was held at the U.S. Air Force Academy's indoor practice facility in Colorado Springs because there had been a snowstorm in Denver. And the Hall of Famer and Broncos executive vice president of football operations remembers one of the first things he bonded over with his backup of nine years, who would become his offensive coordinator for the final four years of his playing career, his friend and confidante for more than 30 years, and, now, the head coach who has fulfilled Elway's mission to get the Broncos back to the Super Bowl.

"The Andy Griffith Show."

"All the old-time sitcoms," Elway said. "We had similar interests in what we liked to watch on TV. There are certain people you get along with. We've never had a cross word. We've never raised our voices or got mad at each other."

Elway and Kubiak and their extraordinary friendship are at the center of Denver's run to this Super Bowl, at least as critical to the Broncos' fortunes as the top-ranked defense and the legendary quarterback who are the team's headliners.

Elway might have hired Kubiak several years ago when he first became the Broncos' top football executive if the Houston Texans hadn't extended Kubiak when many expected him to be fired following the 2010 season. Elway did choose Kubiak after the 2014 season, which Kubiak had spent coaching the offense in Baltimore. Elway, informed by his own late-career success with a powerful running game, wanted a more balanced offense to ease the responsibility on Peyton Manning — and he knew such an evolution might be fraught with tumult.

Elway trusted not only Kubiak's offensive system built on stretch runs, bootlegs and rollouts, but the easy-going manner that Elway has seen up close since Kubiak backed him up, to steady the Broncos through the sensitive decisions that would be threaded through the season.

Elway is unquestionably the franchise's alpha executive who has positioned the Broncos to play with an aging quarterback and then to play without him, but it is Kubiak, the detail-driven studier most comfortable out of the spotlight,

who had the fist-wrapped-in-a-velvet-glove touch with players that managed the tricky dynamics this season.

This is part of why it worked so well this season.

"I don't think you'll find a single player inside football that doesn't like Gary Kubiak. Even guys he cuts," said Houston Texans defensive lineman J.J. Watt, who played for Kubiak when he was Houston's head coach. "He's just an incredibly genuine, nice, caring, good man. He does have a bit more of a laid-back style. He lets players do their thing."

During those years in Houston, Kubiak once made a comment to a Texans staffer that seemed to sum up his coaching philosophy.

"They've got to know that you care before they care what you know."

"I would hope they'd say I'm honest with them," Kubiak said referring to his players – past and present. "I think that's the biggest thing. Players are smart. They've worked hard to get to the National Football League level. There are no shortcuts around being successful in our business and doing it the right way. I just try to be honest with them, be fair to them."

"Listen, anytime you have a quarterback situation where more than one plays, there's going to be a controversy," Broncos defensive coordinator Wade Phillips said. "Gary has taken that out of it. It's pretty amazing what he's done. You have a Hall of Fame player, then another guy plays and then he plays well and then he puts the Hall of Famer back in. He's honest. He has talked to them first, and been honest with the team. *'This is what is going on, this is what we'll do.'* "

All they have done is win. If Manning and the Broncos can win once more in Super Bowl 50, it would be Denver's first championship since Kubiak helped guide Elway into retirement as a champion. The man behind the curtain then, the coach who is uncomfortable with the spotlight, might finally find it shining on him. ∎

Coach Kubiak kids around with Demaryius Thomas during Super Bowl 50 media day. *AP Photo*

SUPER BOWL CHAMPIONS

Denver cornerback Aqib Talib (21) send New England quarterback Tom Brady (12) airborne with this fourth quarter tackle. *AP Photo*

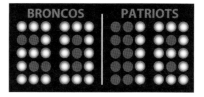

BRONCOS | PATRIOTS

**vs. New England Patriots, Jan. 24
Sports Authority Field at Mile High
Denver, Colorado**

BRONCOS HEADED TO SUPER BOWL 50

Peyton Manning threw two touchdown passes to tight end Owen Daniels and Denver's defense came up with three critical stops late in the fourth quarter as the Broncos beat the New England Patriots 20-18 Sunday to advance to their second Super Bowl in three years.

Manning outdueled Tom Brady in their fabled rivalry with a huge assist from the defense, led by linebacker Von Miller's 2.5 sacks and interception.

Manning's third-quarter scramble for a first down — or as he called it "the run," — might be the most celebrated scramble by a Broncos quarterback since John Elway helicoptered in the Super Bowl 18 years ago. It was certainly the most unexpected.

"Peyton's going to do what he has to do to win," Broncos coach Gary Kubiak said. "He's one of the greatest competitors ever in this league."

Trailing by eight at halftime, the Patriots pulled to within 17-12 on kicker Stephen Gostkowski's second field goal, a 38-yarder with 10:38 remaining in third quarter.

Denver managed to add a field goal by Brandon McManus, a 31-yarder with 10:02 left to play after Manning slightly overthrew wide receiver Jordan Norwood in the center of the end zone on 3rd-and-goal from the 13.

Down by eight and facing 4th-and-1 at the Broncos' 16 with 5:56 left, the Patriots passed up the field goal try. But Brady's pass in the flat to wide receiver Danny Amendola was stopped for a one-yard loss.

Broncos linebacker Von Miller (58) celebrates with teammates after intercepting a pass from Patriots quarterback Tom Brady.
AP Photo

After forcing a Denver punt the Patriots took over at their own 29 with 4:35 remaining. Again, Brady moved the Patriots downfield, getting a big chunk with a 28-yard pass to tight end Rob Gronkowski.

But facing a fourth and 6 from Denver's 14-yard line with 2:18 remaining, the Patriots again went for it and Brady, backpedaling and under duress by Denver's pass rush, threw incomplete to the triple-covered Gronkowski in the end zone.

In a game that would ultimately come down to one play, Patriots coach Bill Belichick's decision to pass on short field goal attempts twice while trailing by eight in the fourth quarter ended up being huge.

"Because of the scoring situation in the game,"

Belichick said postgame when asked about those decisions.

Denver again was held without a first down and the Patriots, using timeouts and the two-minute warning, got the ball back at midfield with 1:52 remaining for one last possession.

On 4th-and-10, Brady threaded the needle between two defenders for a 40-yard completion to Gronkowski to set up a first and goal at the 10.

Wide receiver Julian Edelman caught a six-yard pass between a pair of incompletions before Gronkowski's leaping touchdown grab over cornerback Chris Harris, pulling the Patriots to within two points with 12 seconds remaining.

Needing a two-point conversion to tie — Gostkowski missed a PAT in the first quarter, his

only miss all season — cornerback Aqib Talib tipped Brady's conversion pass and it was intercepted by cornerback Bradley Roby.

Broncos backup safety Shilo Keo recovered the ensuing onside kick for the Broncos to seal the win.

Brady, who was harassed all day by the Denver defense, was 27 of 56 for 310 yards with one

Broncos quarterback Peyton Manning (18) drills a seam pass that is caught by tight end Owen Daniels (81), inset, for a 21-yard touchdown. *AP Photo*

New England quarterback Tom Brady was under constant pressure the entire day from the Broncos defense. Brady was sacked four times and hit 16 other times by the relentless Denver defense. *AP Photo*

Broncos tight end Owen Daniels (81) stays in bounds as he hauls in a 12-yard touchdown pass in the corner of the end zone. Daniels beat Patriots linebacker Jaime Collins (91), right, on the play. *AP Photo*

Denver cornerbacks Chris Harris Jr. (25) and Aqib Talib (21) stop Patriots receiver Julian Edelman dead in his tracks on a key 4th-and- 1 play during the fourth quarter. *AP Photo*

score and two interceptions for a passer rating of 56.4.

Manning was 17-for-32 for 176 yards. Not vintage Manning, but 17 completions were enough, and the two most important were touchdowns to Owen Daniels, the tight end who has played his whole career with Kubiak.

"He understands where he is and what we're trying to do offensively," Elway said of his veteran QB, who has a chance to walk off a champion, like No. 7 did. "He has always been a great game manager, but even more so now."

Miller, playing perhaps his best game as a Bronco, helped give Denver an early lead.

Dropping into coverage instead of rushing the passer, the Broncos' linebacker intercepted a Brady pass intended for Gronkowski and returned it four yards to the Patriots' 16-yard line. Two plays later, Daniels slipped past linebacker Jamie Collins with a double move and Manning lofted a pass from 12 yards out that Daniels caught up with in the corner of the end zone.

McManus drilled a 52-yard field goal in the final moments of the second quarter giving Denver a 17-9 halftime lead.

The Patriots won a replay review to help set up their initial touchdown when it was determined that Manning's pass in the flat to running back Ronnie Hillman, at first ruled incomplete, had traveled backward, allowing linebacker Jonathan Freeny's recovery of the loose ball at the Broncos' 22-yard line to stand.

Running back Brandon Bolden turned a short

Broncos cornerback Aqib Talib (21) and safety Shiloh Keo break up a 4th down pass intended for Patriots tight end Rob Gronkowski. *AP Photo*

▲Patriots tight end Rob Gronkowski (87) catches a 4-yard touchdown pass late in the fourth quarter while being defended by Broncos cornerback Chris Harris Jr. (25). *AP Photo*

▶Two of the all-time greats – Peyton Manning and Tom Brady – shake hands following the Broncos win in the AFC Championship game. *AP Photo*

pass from Brady into a 20-yard gain and a subsequent personal foul penalty set up a first and goal at the 1. Stephen Jackson scored on the next play but Gostkowski missed the extra point wide right that would prove costly.

"All day, these guys put their bodies and lives on the line, and for me to come out here and miss a kick, it's a nightmare scenario," Gostkowski said.

And now the strangest season of Manning's Hall of Fame career will play itself out in Santa Clara, California at Super Bowl 50.

"It's been a unique season," Manning said. "And this game today was a unique football game. I've really tried to take it one week at a time all season long, through the injuries and all the things that have gone on, I've stayed in the moment, stayed patient. That's served me well."∎

BOX SCORE

	1	2	3	4	T
New England	6	3	3	6	18
Denver	7	10	0	3	20

SCORING SUMMARY

FIRST QUARTER
DEN　TD　7:32　Owen Daniels 21 Yd pass from Peyton Manning (Brandon McManus Kick)
Drive info: 11 plays, 83 yards, 5:30

NE　TD　1:49　Steven Jackson 1 Yd Run
Drive info: 2 plays, 22 yards, 0:34

SECOND QUARTER
DEN　TD　13:46　Owen Daniels 21 Yd pass from Peyton Manning (Brandon McManus Kick)
Drive info: 3 plays, 16 yards, 0:49

NE　FG　7:02　Stephen Gostkowski 46 Yd Field Goal
Drive info: 11 plays, 62 yards, 3:14

DEN　FG　0:33　Brandon McManus 52 Yd Field Goal
Drive info: 6 plays, 23 yards, 1:13

THIRD QUARTER
NE　FG　7:02　Stephen Gostkowski 46 Yd Field Goal
Drive info: 8 plays, 47 yards, 2:49

FOURTH QUARTER
DEN　FG　10:02　Brandon McManus 31 Yd Field Goal
Drive info: 10 plays, 48 yards, 4:58

NE　TD　0:12　Rob Gronkowski 4 Yd pass from Tom Brady (Two-Point Pass Conversion Failed)
Drive info: 8 plays, 50 yards, 1:40

GAME LEADERS

PASSING YARDS
NE　T. Brady　27-56, 310 YDS, 1 TD, 2 INT
DEN　P. Manning　17-32, 176 YDS, 2 TD

RUSHING YARDS
NE　T. Brady　3 CAR, 13 YDS
DEN　C.J. Anderson　16 CAR, 72 YDS

RECEIVING YARDS
NE　R. Gronkowski　8 REC, 144 YDS, 1 TD
DEN　E. Sanders　5 REC, 62 YDS

Denver general manager and executive vice president of football operations John Elway, left, holds the AFC Championship trophy as head coach Gary Kubiak looks on. *AP Photo*

Captions from left: The Broncos team plane arrives in California where they are greeted by Super Bowl legend Terrell Davis. *AP Photo*

Peyton Manning is swarmed by the media at the inaugural Super Bowl 50 Opening Night. *AP Photo*

The Vince Lomardi Trophy. *AP Photo*

SUPER BOWL CHAMPIONS

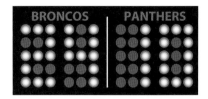

BRONCOS | **PANTHERS**

**vs. Carolina Panthers, Feb. 7
Levi's Stadium
Santa Clara, California**

WORLD CHAMPIONS!

BRONCOS D DOMINATES CAROLINA IN SUPER BOWL 50

Every Superman has his kryptonite. For Cam Newton in Super Bowl 50, his name was Von Miller.

As quarterback Peyton Manning predicted all week long leading up to the game the Denver defense relentlessly chased and knocked around the newly named league MVP.

And much like the rest of their season, Manning had just enough left in his 39-year-old body to keep things in order on offense and give the Broncos' defense room to stomp, flex and rumble to a 24-10 win over the Carolina Panthers in Super Bowl 50 at Levi's Stadium.

"I'm just glad I'm on the same team as our defense and glad I don't have to play against them ... No question our defense led the way," Manning said.

The victory is the Broncos' third in the Super Bowl — it was the team's record-tying eighth trip — and ultimately fulfilled a promise Broncos general manager John Elway made to Manning in 2012.

Broncos linebacker Von Miller (58) strips the ball from Carolina quarterback Cam Newton (1) resulting in a fumble that rolled into the end zone where it was recovered by Denver for a touchdown. *AP Photo*

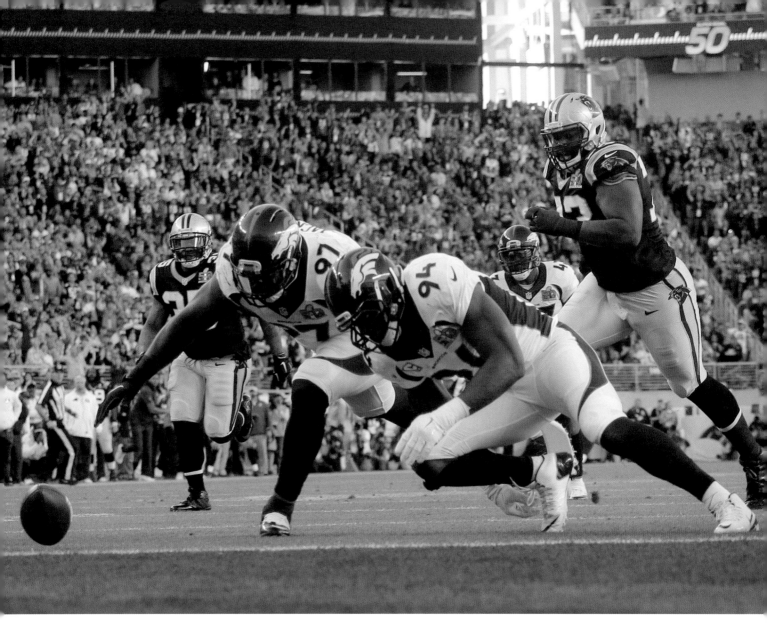

Broncos Malik Jackson (97) and DeMarcus Ware (94) chase after a first quarter fumble that rolled into the end zone. Panthers quarterback Cam Newton lost the ball when he was stripped by Broncos linebacker Von Miller. Jackson ended up recovering the ball for the touchdown and a 10-0 Denver lead. *AP Photo*

Elway told Manning he would do "everything in my power," to help him close out his career with a championship. That everything included giving the Broncos the kind of defense Manning has never had in tow before.

Defensive coordinator Wade Phillips has said the Broncos' cornerbacks are the best he has had in his almost four decades' worth of work in the NFL. They are the kind of defensive backs the pass-rushers love because they give them the time they need to get home.

And Phillips has consistently described linebacker Miller as "special."

From the moment Miller arrived in Denver with

the second pick of the 2011 draft, his coveted ability to turn speed to power, power to speed has been on display. But when DeMarcus Ware arrived in free agency in 2014 it transitioned Miller from gifted athlete to full-blown football hell-raiser with the drive, moves and down-to-down determination to lead a defense to a Super Bowl win.

"Me and my teammates and all my guys. This is what you work for," Miller said. "I am so proud of my buddies. I am so proud of my teammates and coaches."

Spearheading the league's top-ranked defense, Miller was all over the field from the outset.

With the Broncos leading 3-0 in the first

Broncos punt returner Jordan Norwood (11) returns a second quarter punt a Super Bowl record 61-yards. *AP Photo*

quarter, Miller got to Newton for a strip-sack. The ball was recovered by defensive end Malik Jackson for the first touchdown of the game and a 10-0 Denver lead.

Miller finished the first half with a sack, a quarterback hit and four tackles, and he was just getting started.

With the Panthers driving to open the third quarter, Miller broke up a pass deep down the right sideline intended for wide receiver Jerricho Cotchery. He later ended another Carolina drive when he beat Panthers right tackle Mike Remmers with a move Miller didn't have early in his career — the spin back inside when the tackle tried to push him out wide.

The Denver offense continued to stall, however, and Coach Gary Kubiak opted for a conservative approach with his team clinging to a 16-10 lead. That included calling three consecutive run plays and punting the ball back to Carolina with 4:55 remaining.

That's when Miller decided to put an exclamation point on the day.

He blew past the beleaguered Remmers and knocked the ball free from Newton in the game's final minutes, showing enough power and leverage to hold off Remmers with one arm and knock the ball out — left-handed — with the other. That play

Quarterback Peyton Manning (18) fires a strike to Emmanuel Sanders (10), inset, who breaks away from Panthers cornerback Robert McClain for a 25-yard gain.
AP Photo

DENVER BRONCOS

Super Bowl MVP Von Miller (58) strips Panthers quarterback Cam Newton (1) for the second time resulting in a fumble that was recovered by the Broncos T.J. Ward. *AP Photo*

led to the Broncos' first offensive touchdown of the game — with 3 minutes, 8 seconds to play — a score that gave the Broncos a 24-10 lead when C.J. Anderson plowed over Panthers Pro Bowl linebacker Luke Kuechly into the end zone.

As a team the Broncos tied a Super Bowl record with seven sacks and pressured Newton a season-high 19 times.

Phillips said he often works back from Miller in the pass-rush plan. Even if Miller doesn't get a sack, the attention offenses must pay him has allowed the Broncos to unleash a diverse pass rush that has powered the defense.

"Von Miller has beat his guy almost every play this season," Phillips said. "When they put other guys over there to help, then we can do some things."

It's why 13 different players had at least one

sack for the Broncos in the regular season. And why when the Panthers tried to add a tight end, move a player to unbalance their front Sunday, the Broncos still generated pressure on Newton.

Carolina's offense was on the field for 32:47, but produced only 315 net yards and 10 points while turning the ball over four times.

"It just shows what type of team we have," Miller said. "It is not about offense, defense or special teams. We came together as a whole. We spent a lot of time together.

"It is a college atmosphere. We have a lot of love for each other, and that is where the success came from."

In the end Manning was right, the Broncos' defense was why the Broncos played for the Lombardi trophy and certainly why they hoisted it. And they made that perfectly clear.∎

The Denver defensive front had Cam Newton on the run all game. The Broncos defense tied a Super Bowl record with seven sacks on the day. *AP Photo*

▲Broncos running back C.J. Anderson powers in for a 2-yard touchdown run with 3:08 left in the game. *AP Photo*

▼Linebacker Danny Trevathan (59) makes a heads up play by recovering the fumble of teammate T.J. Ward (43). Ward had just intercepted a pass when he was hit and lost the ball. *AP Photo*

Broncos receiver Bennie Fowler (16) celebrates after catching a clutch 2-point conversion late in the fourth quarter. *AP Photo*

BOX SCORE

	1	2	3	4	T
Carolina	0	7	0	3	10
Denver	10	3	3	8	24

SCORING SUMMARY

FIRST QUARTER
DEN FG 10:43 Brandon McManus 34 Yd Field Goal
Drive info: 10 plays, 64 yards, 4:17

DEN TD 6:27 Malik Jackson fumble recovery in end zone (Brandon McManus Kick)
Drive info: 3 plays, -15 yards, 0:56

SECOND QUARTER
CAR TD 11:25 Jonathan Stewart 1 Yd Run (Graham Gano Kick)
Drive info: 9 plays, 73 yards, 4:50

DEN FG 6:58 Brandon McManus 33 Yd Field Goal
Drive info: 4 plays, -1 yards, 2:13

THIRD QUARTER
DEN FG 8:18 Brandon McManus 30 Yd Field Goal
Drive info: 7 plays, 54 yards, 2:30

FOURTH QUARTER
CAR FG 10:21 Graham Gano 39 Yd Field Goal
Drive info: 6 plays, 29 yards, 2:56

DEN TD 3:08 C.J. Anderson 2 Yd Run (Peyton Manning Pass to Bennie Fowler for Two-Point Coversion)
Drive info: 3 plays, 4 yards, 0:56

GAME LEADERS

PASSING YARDS
CAR C. Newton 18-41, 265 YDS, 1 INT
DEN P. Manning 13-23, 141 YDS, 1 INT

RUSHING YARDS
CAR C. Newton 6 CAR, 45 YDS
DEN C.J. Anderson 23 CAR, 90 YDS, 1 TD

RECEIVING YARDS
CAR C. Brown 4 REC, 80 YDS
DEN E. Sanders 6 REC, 83 YDS

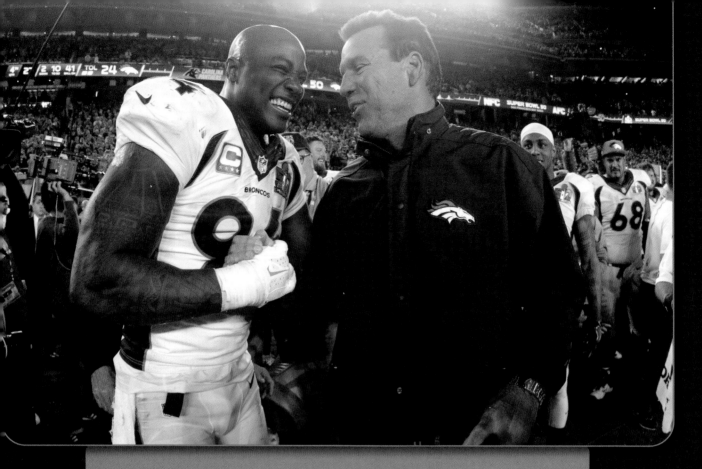

▲DeMarcus Ware (94) and head coach Gary Kubiak celebrate after their win. *AP Photo*

▼Broncos players – Louis Vasquez, Ryan Harris and Evan Mathis – take part in the post game celebration. *AP Photo*

Broncos Von Miller holds the Lombardi trophy after winning Super Bowl 50. Miller was named MVP of the game. *AP Photo*

Peyton celebrates with perhaps the next great Manning quarterback – his son, Marshall. *AP Photo*

DENVER BRONCOS